SUNDAY HOMILIES

SUNDAY HOMILIES

CYCLE B

Herbert F. Smith, SJ

ALBA · HOUSE   NEW · YORK

SOCIETY OF ST. PAUL, 2187 VICTORY BLVD., STATEN ISLAND, NEW YORK 10314

ST PAULS

Library of Congress Cataloging-in-Publication Data

Smith, Herbert F.
    Sunday homilies. Cycle B / Herbert F. Smith.
    p. cm.
    ISBN: 0-8189-0597-2
    1. Church year sermons. 2. Catholic Church—Sermons. 3. Sermons,
American. I. Title.
    BX1756.S595S862 1990   90-44789
    252'.6—dc20   CIP

Imprimi Potest:
James A. Devereux, SJ

Nihil Obstat:
Msgr. Thomas J. Herron
Censor Librorum

Imprimatur:
✠ Anthony Bevilacqua, JCD
Archbishop of Philadelphia
May 14, 1990

The Nihil Obstat and Imprimatur are official declarations that a book or pamphlet
is free of doctrinal or moral error. No implication is contained therein that those
who have granted the Nihil Obstat and Imprimatur agree with the contents,
opinions or statements expressed.

Produced and designed in the United States of America by the
Fathers and Brothers of the Society of St. Paul,
2187 Victory Boulevard, Staten Island, New York 10314-6603,
as part of their communications apostolate.

ISBN: 0-8189-0597-2

Printing Information:

Current Printing - first digit   2   3   4   5   6   7   8   9   10

Year of Current Printing - first year shown

              2002 2003 2004 2005 2006 2007 2008 2009 2010

CONTENTS
Cycle B

FOREWORD
George A. Maloney, S.J.

Anthony Trollope, in his novel *Barchester Towers,* writes: "There is perhaps no greater hardship at present inflicted on mankind in civilized and free countries than the necessity of listening to sermons." We priests might wish to amend this statement: "There is perhaps no greater hardship at present inflicted on priests than the necessity of preparing sermons."

What makes it so onerous to prepare good sermons and what makes it so boring for the faithful in the pews to listen to poorly prepared sermons centers chiefly around two elements: the message given and the messenger delivering the message. Jesus realized — and all modern Christians can agree with Him — that the message of the Gospel can be accepted only if both the messenger or preacher of the Word and the listeners not only have a desire to accept the message, but actually incorporate the sermon or homily into their daily lives.

Both need to listen attentively, not only with the mind or intellect, but with the heart. The heart, Blaise Pascal wrote, has its own reasons. The hearts of the preacher and the listeners must be enkindled by the fire of the Holy Spirit to surrender lovingly to the spoken Word and to incorporate that Word into their daily lives as a transforming, living Word.

Another reason for bored listeners and boring preachers is the redundancy of the message preached. We all have heard it before, or so we think! What original thought can be added to the pat formulas we all have traditionally heard in sermons?

But the greatest problem about the message of the Word of God lies equally in the heart of the preacher and of his listeners. Who really wants to change? Why not all agree on sweet, soothing sentiments in sermons because it is so much a struggle to live more radically the Gospel than to hear it and walk away unchanged?

The preacher personally faces many problems in his struggle to prevent boredom that lulls his listeners into lethargy rather than to release lightning bolts from the firmaments. Is he a man of deep prayer who builds his spiritual life on the Word of God as revealed in the Old and New Testaments, imaged most perfectly in the risen Jesus, who dwells within him as the living Speech of God?

Has he kept up with biblical research and modern psychology? Is he in touch with the problems facing his congregation or is he preaching to faceless people out of a medieval understanding of the Word of God? Before a priest can lead others into the presence of God, he must listen to God's Word. If a priest preaches before he has listened to the Word of God, he will be as St. Paul says: ". . . sounding brass and tinkling cymbal." If a priest celebrates the death and resurrection of Jesus Christ before he has experienced his own death to self and a new life to Christ, he will be only a cultic minister of valid sacraments, but he will fail to usher others into the awesome "mysterium."

We priests will eagerly find time to pray and preach from Scripture if we realize that through God's written Word we enter into a mysterious and wonderful communication between God and ourselves. We become his privileged children as Vatican II's decree on *Divine Revelation* (#21) phrases it:

> In the sacred books the Father who is in heaven comes lovingly to meet his children and talks with them. And such is the force and power of the Word of God that it serves the Church as her support and vigor, and it

provides the children of the Church strength for their faith, food for the soul and a pure and lasting fount of spiritual life. Scripture verifies in the most perfect way the words: "The Word of God is living and active" (Heb 4:12) and is "able to build you up and to give you the inheritance among all those who are sanctified" (Ac 20:32; 1 Th 2:13).

In preaching retreats to priests, but also to religious and laity, I find today a great hunger among many to meet Jesus Christ as Lord and Savior in the immediacy of deeper prayer in the Spirit. They are turning to commentaries on the revealed books of Holy Scripture. Priests, but also the laity, are searching for insights from homiletic commentaries for preaching, for teaching religion, and as an aid to personal and group prayer.

I highly recommend this present volume of homilies written by Fr. Herbert F. Smith, S.J. on the readings for the Sundays of the B Cycle, including also his already published *Sunday Homilies: Cycle A* (Alba House, 1989). In Father Smith we are treated to a spiritual messenger well skilled in preaching through his retreats and sermons. His insights are solidly based on Scripture and a living, experiential theology. He evidently is a most prayerful priest for whom the Lord is real and daily is experienced by him in his own prayer and in his apostolate, chiefly that of preaching and writing books and articles on the spiritual life.

Most readers will appreciate his discipline to develop — with an economy of words, meaningful quotes and examples — all three readings of a given Sunday or major feast during the liturgical year. His years of scriptural studies give him an ease in dealing with the history of salvation that never gets lost in sheer scholarship divorced from the lives of his readers. The text of both these volumes shimmers with delicate insights, expressed in beautiful prose that comes out of the author's personal experience with living God's revealed word.

He is grounded in the traditional teachings of the Church, yet is up-to-date and stretches always to find new ways of expressing the "old" in something new that resonates with the lives of ordinary Christians in the modern world. He so simply packs each 2½ to 3 page homily with a richness of scholarship and heart-language that the reader is challenged to an ongoing conversion to "eat" the Word of God (in the words of St. Ignatius of Antioch) and to witness to the living Word experienced through this most gracious, humble and Spirit-filled messenger of the Good News. These two volumes on the Sunday readings of Cycles A and B provide a treasure-trove of insights and inspiration for all priests seeking knowledge of the mind and of the heart as they prepare for their Sunday challenge to preach a Spirit-filled sermon. They will also be a source of great wealth to all other Christians wishing to prepare the soil of their heart to receive the Word of God each Sunday and to bring forth another hundredfold.

SUNDAY HOMILIES

ANOTHER KIND OF WAITING

Today we begin a new year in our religious life and our worship. We start preparing for the Lord's birthday. But we prepare for more than that. We prepare for all his comings.

Even unbelievers have begun searching for the right Christmas gifts for their loved ones. We for our part have to remember the most loved one of all, our Lord Jesus Christ. What is the choicest gift for him? We needn't shop for it, nor do we have to think what it should be. He gave us himself, and he wants from us our very selves.

Advent is the time of preparing the gift of self for Christ. Shouldn't we prepare as earnestly to profit spiritually from this season as commercial interests do to make money? They've already gotten started. Our preparation involves looking back, looking to the present, and looking forward. The three readings help us do it.

In the first reading the people of God are pleading to God to come to their aid. They're back from the foreign land where their conquerors exiled them. They thought it would be all roses at home in Israel. But in fact things are a mess. They feel dirtied by their sins, shamed by their betrayals, and justly abandoned to their troubles. They're lonely for God and his help, and so they call out to him: "Rend the heavens and come down! Do unheard of wonders! Complete the work of your hands!" In a word, they call on God to come as their Lord and Savior.

By the time of the second reading, written several hundred years later, their cry had been answered. God the Son had torn open the heavens and come down in the Incarnation. The Virgin Mary had conceived, Christ had been born on the first Christmas, and his resurrection had taken place. The first Christians had been called, and we are hearing from them through St. Paul.

Paul's point is: Don't settle for what Christ has already done. Look forward to his return. Keep serving with your wonderful gifts so you'll be free of blame and eager for his second coming.

In the Gospel, our Lord's parable tells us the kind of waiting we must do. Two thousand years have passed. He has come in many ways with gifts and graces for his people, but his final coming has not yet taken place, for all is not yet ready.

On the other hand, the Lord has come personally to all who have lived and died before us. For, after all, death is Christ's final coming to each individual called home before the Lord's second coming. So, his parable applies both to his coming to call us individually, and to his coming to call home the whole human race.

Our Advent worship of waiting, then, is really a waiting for all the comings of God into our lives. We meditate on his past comings; we alert ourselves to his daily comings into our lives; we look to the celebration of his birthday; and we prepare for his final coming and our going home to him.

So this "Advent waiting" is a very special kind of waiting, as our Lord's parable makes evident. I can describe this waiting in several words. It is an *active* waiting. It's not like standing at a bus stop, where you can do nothing but fidget until the bus comes. It's a waiting of preparation, a waiting by doing, a waiting by making everything ready for the Master's return.

In the parable, the householder's employees and family wait by carrying out their responsibilities faithfully. They wait by preparing everything so that all will be in order when the head of the house returns. Then his arrival will be a happy affair for everybody; otherwise it will not be.

The parable is a guide for our Advent waiting. We make a special effort to conduct ourselves as Jesus wants. The Scriptures even tell us that we can speed up the desired second coming of

Jesus by completing the work that must be done on earth. Our waiting, then, is not passive but active.

This waiting is sometimes a *painful* waiting. As we saw in that first reading, things were not going right. The people were suffering. As Jesus told us, we too will suffer. The world takes a dim view of moral truths and responsibilities. It doesn't want to be reminded of them even by seeing us live them. Besides that, we have our own failings and sins. They are our worst sufferings. But our very suffering is preparation. It's our share in Christ's redemptive cross; and it makes us long the more for his return.

Our waiting is also *progressive*. Unlike the people of old, we no longer have to await Jesus' Incarnation and resurrection. Furthermore, Jesus keeps coming in many ways. He visits us through life's events, through prayer, and through sacrament. At this Mass he will rend the heavens and come down to us. But we must be alert, or we won't recognize these comings. Think of the people who lived during his time on earth and never recognized him. Advent is meant to make us more sensitive to the many ways the Lord keeps coming into our lives.

This waiting is *communicative*. We don't wait as though God is far away like a bus out of sight. By prayer, we talk to God already present, and beg him to become more present. We wait to be fully with him, as love desires.

This waiting is also *penitential*. We search our lives for the obstacles to his coming, find them, and remove them. We correct what's wrong, stir sorrow for our sins, and confess them. We pray more, go to Mass more, and help others more. We do whatever we can to intensify our love life with God.

In summary: Advent preparation is self-preparation. Christmas giving is self-giving. Advent is the season of faith in what God has done for us, and of hope in what he will do.

When the spiritually wise make a reflection like this they summarize it in a pithy phrase they can call prayerfully to mind throughout the day. They call the phrase a mystical formula or a mantra. I call it a spiritual capsule. I'll prescribe one which you can take as often each day as you like. It is the second last verse of the whole Bible, and it is perfect for Advent. Our spiritual capsule, then, is *Come, Lord Jesus!*

"ABC" — Immaculate Conception   Gn 3:9-15, 20
                                                        Ep 1:3-6, 11-12
                                                        Lk 1:26-38

THE IMMACULATE CONCEPTION AND US

Sensible salespeople show promising customers their best products. Proud artists hang their finest paintings in the most prominent places. Christ the divine Artist of redemption has adopted a similar strategy. Our Blessed Lady is the masterpiece of his redemptive work, so he features her in Scripture and tradition to make us, too, long to be saved by him.

And so Holy Mother the Church, who has Mary as her Mother, calls us to honor Mary at the beginning of this new liturgical year. With joy we celebrate this great feast of her Immaculate Conception. Though words can't measure up to this mystery, let's try to grasp it as best we can.

What is the Immaculate Conception? How do we share in it? How do we imitate Mary?

In the old quarter of Jerusalem where the ancient temple stood there hangs on a weathered door the placard, "The Virgin Mary was born here." It could have been on that very spot, then, that the mystery we celebrate today took place. In the courtyard behind that old building is the great Church of St. Ann. This mystery has to do with St. Ann, Mary's mother, and St. Joachim, her father, together with God the Father, Son and Holy Spirit.

To really grasp the mystery, we have to go back to the fall of Adam and Eve. That is why the Church reads the account of the fall today at Mass. Our first parents lost their share in the divine nature through disobedience and could not pass it on to their children. And so, one after the other, human beings were born into this world deprived of eternal life.

The good news is that even in the hour of the fall God promised a Redeemer. As the ages passed, the Chosen People longed for his coming. Then came Joachim and Ann. They fell in love and married. They expressed their marital love in the normal way, and Ann conceived a girl-child who would be called Mary.

But here we stop and gaze into the mystery. At the very moment Ann conceived, God intervened in a special way. He blocked the flow of original sin. He poured into Mary's soul the grace of the divine likeness which had not been seen on earth since it was lost by Adam and Eve.

What then is the Immaculate Conception? It is the coming into being of Mary through the love-making of her parents plus a divine intervention that began the work of our redemption.

Each of us is a conception, begotten by our father, conceived by our mother. So each of us can say, "I am a conception"; but only Mary can say as she did at Lourdes, "I am the Immaculate Conception," that is, the stainless Conception.

In defining the dogma of the Immaculate Conception, Pope Pius IX said, "The most Blessed Virgin Mary, from the first moment of her conception was, by the singular grace and privilege of Almighty God, in view of the merits of Christ Jesus the Savior of the human race, preserved immune from all stain of original sin." Mary, then, is the Immaculate Conception.

How do we share in the Immaculate Conception? We must share in it, because if the Immaculate Conception is the beginning of the redemption of one person then it has to be repeated in some way to redeem each person. And it is. Jesus said to Nicodemus, "No one can enter the kingdom of God without being born of water and Spirit.'' At baptism we were reborn as God's children, and all our sins were taken away. In a sense, we are belated Immaculate Conceptions. If we died immediately after baptism, we would go straight to heaven. So we do share to a degree in the Immaculate Conception of Mary, who is our Mother in the life of God.

When one priest was describing our rebirth, a very smart little child said, ''How can God be my Father?'' The priest said, ''You mean because you already have a father?'' He said, ''Yes,'' and the priest explained how God became his Father in baptism by giving him a share in the divine nature that made him like God. Interiorly, in his soul, he became an image and likeness of God. And so did we all when we were baptized.

Thirdly, how do we imitate Mary? For if we are her children, do we not have to imitate her as every child imitates his parents? It is easy to put Mary on a pedestal, but we honor her far more honestly by patterning our lives after hers.

St. Alphonsus Liguori tells the story of a young man who used to kneel at a statue of Our Lady with seven swords in her heart. One night he committed serious sin. The next time he knelt, he saw Our Lady now had eight swords in her heart. Then and there he must have found out that he had to show his love by imitating her sinlessness, for she loved him.

We may think it's too difficult to imitate Mary's holiness, but let me remind you we even have to imitate Jesus' own holiness. He said, ''I am the Way.'' If we can imitate him, who is the God-man, we can certainly imitate Our Lady. And we began at baptism. God starts the imitation for us. In that powerful second reading St. Paul says that God chose us in Christ to be ''holy and without blemish before him.'' That's almost a description of the Immaculate Mary, but it's about us as well.

We're not really good Christians until we try to live wholly without blemish. The purpose of our life is to gradually recover that holiness which Adam and Eve had and which Mary was given at the moment of her Immaculate Conception and never lost. Our

Lord even said, "You must become perfect as your Heavenly Father is perfect." So let us imitate Mary's selfless love and her sinlessness. Sinlessness consists in keeping God's law, so let us imitate Mary's eagerness to do all God commands and all he asks.

Few people ever become such close friends as those who labor together as comrades in some great and noble cause. Our Lady was the comrade of our Lord in that sense. She labored with him for the most noble work which ever took place in this world, the work of redemption. We can imitate Our Lady in that. Let us not just keep the law of God to save our own skins, but labor with Jesus and Mary day in and day out for the redemption of the world.

In her last recorded words Mary said, "Do whatever He tells you." If we love her and love God we will try to do exactly that. When we receive the Son of God and Mary in Holy Communion today let us say to him, "Be it done to me as you desire."

"B" — Second Sunday of Advent
Is 40:1-5, 9-11
2 P 3:8-14
Mk 1:1-8

MARY AND JOHN PREPARE THE WAY

"Say to the cities of Judah, Here is your God!" That is what the feast of Christmas says to us: "Here is your God!" But to reach Christmas we have to ascend the weeks of Advent. We have to pass beyond the mountains and valleys and rugged lands of our lives. If we fail, we may reach Christmas as a date in the calendar, but not as the feast of Emmanuel, God-with-us.

The Virgin Mary and her kinsman John the Baptist prepared the way of the Lord. We must observe and imitate them to prepare his way into our own lives. Mary, in her Immaculate Conception, was the Morning Star rising in history. When the morning star appears, we know that the sun itself will soon rise in the east. And indeed Christ, the Light of the World, was soon born of the Virgin Mary.

The theme of Mary as preparer of the way of the Lord is captured in the lovely hymn:

> Mary the dawn, Christ the Perfect Day;
> Mary the gate, Christ the Heavenly Way!
> Mary the root, Christ the Mystic Vine;
> Mary the grape, Christ the Sacred Wine! . . .
> Mary the mother, Christ the mother's Son
> By all things blest while endless ages run. Amen.

Mary prepared the way for the Lord on the first Christmas. If we turn to her for help she will prepare his way into our lives this Christmas.

Let us look at the hindrances to Christ which must be removed in our lives, the hindrances which must be removed in family life, and the solutions we find by imitating Mary and John the Baptist.

Isaiah singled out the hindrances to be eliminated from our lives. The mountains must be leveled. We can see them as the high peaks of selfishness and greed which hem us in and cut off the view of God and of all whom we want to love more faithfully. This Advent we have to blast away our selfishness with the spiritual dynamite of prayer. Nearby are the valleys of neglect of duties. We will fill them in by acts of faithfulness and love. There in the distance are the rough ways of wasted time and excessive TV and all the junk-activities we have admitted into our lives. The new schedule we draw up will make a smooth path for the Lord to enter in their place.

We must also remove the hindrances from family life. What are they? You will best see what they are if you compare family life to a juggling act. Picture a talent contest at your local theater. Ten families stand in groups on the stage. Each family is given a vase which must be tossed from one family member to another. Most manage to do it without breakage. But then a cup and saucer are added, and then a wedding ring and a crucifix and a doll. By now crashes are heard on all sides. At first there is laughter, but then cries of pain as the contestants step on shards of broken glass.

Perhaps the symbolism is already clear to you. Married life is a juggling act. Families let more and more activities enter their lives until finally all the family members are jugglers trying to keep it all in the air. But you know what happens. Often the best things fall and break. Perhaps the crucifix falls and breaks. They have broken their relationship to God. Then the wedding ring falls and breaks. The marriage is on the rocks. Then the doll falls and breaks. That is the child wounded by divorce.

But there is one family on the stage that has won the contest. They made a judgment early. They saw they couldn't keep all the items going, so they threw out the vase and cup and saucer, and kept in the air only the wedding ring and crucifix and doll. What a round of applause they're receiving!

When we add too many items to the juggling act of our lives, the very best may fall and get broken. It's an old story. The French author Gustave Flaubert described it in the last century, in his novel *Madame Bovary*. She was married to a workaholic husband. She was a spendthrift wife. He blamed her for the spending that drove him to work harder, and she blamed him for the work habits that drove her in her loneliness to spend more. They ended in disaster.

More recently, the *Wall Street Journal* described the Wall Street Widow, the wife whose husband is married more to his company than to her. That's the way Madame Bovary felt. But now the *Wall Street Journal* should be describing the Wall Street Orphan, the child whose parents are both married more to their companies than to one another.

One priest who was preparing a homily on this topic was reading an article about a successful business tycoon. He read the words, "He is a self-confessed workaholic," and said, "Oh, Oh!" The next paragraph began, "His six-year marriage . . . dissolved recently."

Let us look at the solutions we find in the lives of Mary and John the Baptist.

Mary teaches us to abandon the juggling act in which we try to stuff everything possible into our lives. She shows the way to a life of love, which is the way of happiness. She holds with all her heart to God and all her loved ones, and has no room in her heart to crave things that count for little. In your Advent prayer, learn from Mary. Make a daily spiritual pilgrimage to her little home in Nazareth. Use your imagination to observe her about the house. Picture her with Jesus and Joseph at supper, and listen in. Learn where true joy can be found.

Then meditate on her kinsman, John the Baptist. When you think your wardrobe has to be expanded, look at him wearing a garment of camel's hair, and decide you have more than enough. When you want a richer diet, watch him eating grasshoppers. Say, "How could anybody eat grasshoppers?" And hear the rabbis tell you that there are 800 edible varieties. Do we really have to spoil ourselves so much? What do we really want? We'd better find out before the juggling act of life turns into the disaster we so often see around us.

Mary and John are both saying clearly, "Life wasn't given any of us to perform a juggling act, but to prepare the way of the Lord." Let our daily spiritual capsule for the week be the prayer, "Mary, help me to prepare the way of my Lord."

CALLED TO JOY

These rose-colored priestly vestments are meant to proclaim the theme of the day. This is Gaudete Sunday, Rejoice-and-be-glad Sunday. Christ brought joy to the world, and we are being brought to Christ.

Joy is the blossom of love, and the Christian religion is woven of love. Today in the readings and in the Church we are instructed in cultivating joy.

In a great sermon by St. Peter Chrysologus we are told how God, seeing the world falling into sin and fear, acted to call it back to him in love. He deluged the world to purge and free it, and called Noah to work with him in love as a partner in ushering in a new era. He called Abraham to a new name and a new role. When Abraham was too old to have hope of fathering a child, God treated him like a son and gave him a son. God cherished Abraham and won his heart and made a covenant with him, so that Abraham worshiped God in love, not fear.

God blessed Abraham's grandson, Jacob, prospered him, and wrestled with him, to teach Jacob not to fear the divine embrace. God called Moses, treated him like a son, and invited him to liberate the people.

These chosen ones, yearning for God and wounded with love of God, wanted to see God with their eyes. They were asking the impossible, St. Peter Chrysologus says, for love has no interest in reason and moderation, but only in love's yearnings. If the lover does not obtain what he loves, he is destroyed by his love.

Then came Mary the Virgin. God filled her with such love that she too must have desired the impossible, desired to see his face. And God, who can do what is impossible to man, became flesh in her womb. She delivered him, she held him in her arms, and she saw God with her own eyes.

This is our joy, that God became flesh and dwelt among us, and we look with joy to celebrating his birthday. In this mystery of God's fulfillment of our desires, joy has blossomed on earth.

In the first reading, we hear of Christ's own joy; in the psalm, of his Virgin Mother's joy; and in the second reading and the Gospel, of the joy we should cultivate.

In the first reading, then, Isaiah speaks in the person of Christ our Lord. Christ comes rejoicing into the world because he is full of justice and righteousness. He is bringing the good news of salvation, and bringing the power to bring it about. He has all the joy of bridegroom and bride on their wedding day.

In the psalm we have Mary crying out her joy in her own Magnificat. She has tasted God's greatness, known blessings that can't be described in words, and witnessed God pouring out his blessings on all the lowly.

St. Paul then gives us an instruction in joy. Paul describes three joy-producing activities which work together and support one another like the three sides of a triangle: Pray, rejoice and give thanks. Do all three without stopping, Paul admonishes us. And don't stifle the spirit, for the spirit infuses our prayer, prayer awakens our joy, and joy inspires us to give thanks. And don't touch anything evil with a ten-foot pole, for evil is the kiss of death to the blossom of love.

Finally, John the Baptist gives us a living example of how to cultivate joy: Give all the credit to Christ the Messiah; take none of it for yourself; recognize that Christ is here now in our midst; and say, "I'm not worthy to unfasten his sandal strap."

The Church adds her instruction in the cultivation of joy. In the opening prayer she has us pray to experience the joy of love and salvation in Christ. Always in the Mass the Church teaches us to make use of the sacraments, for the sacraments are what lead us to Christmas; the sacraments are what lead us to Christ our joy.

If during Advent we do well to confess our sins and seek forgiveness, then the sacrament of reconciliation is the perfect manner of doing it, for in it Christ himself promises the grace of forgiveness.

We may not find confession easy, but at least we don't need the courage manifested by Damien the Leper. When he lived on the island of Molokai, he heard the confessions of others, but there was no priest to hear his own. One day a ship with a priest aboard lay in the harbor. Damien could not get aboard, so from a little skiff he called out his sins across the water and made his confession before all present.

The Church calls us to the humility of love, but also to love's boldness. She teaches us we are not worthy to touch Christ's sandal strap; she leads us to make our confession. She knows we still feel unworthy, but she boldly sends us to embrace Christ in the Eucharist and to plead with him for that holiness and love which are the true preparation for Christmas.

Note in this boldness the unreasonableness of love, which refuses to be channeled by patterns of logic. Here we are confessing our unworthiness to touch Christ's sandal strap, and yet we make bold to embrace him in the Eucharist to find worthiness. We can indeed be accused of being illogical, but we are in fact practicing the higher logic of love, for it is only union with Christ that can ever take away our unworthiness of union with Christ. For union with Christ alone inflames us with the love that alone makes us worthy of Christ.

Love is a kind of law to itself. That is why the only love that will ever keep us completely free from sin is the love of God above all things. The love of God has in it no enticement to evil. When we love God above all we will have the joy of doing whatever we will, for love of God wills to be with God the Beloved and like God the Beloved, and that is the fullness of joy.

"B" — Fourth Sunday of Advent   2 S 7:1-5, 8-11, 16
                                                 Rm 16:25-27
                                                 Lk 1:26-38

THE MESSIANIC MYSTERY UNFOLDS

Many of us are preparing with joy and happiness for the birthday of Christ. Others of us, as any priest would know, are experiencing the pressing griefs and sorrows and troubles of life that even the Advent season doesn't suppress. That makes lived faith a hard struggle. Yet wouldn't you agree that, theoretically at least, we should for love of God count such a struggle as nothing? It is our share in the suffering of Christ, and in the end it will be as nothing, because Christ will call us beyond all struggle to endless joy with him. I hope you agree with me that this is the way we should be, even if in our weakness we are not. St. Paul, for instance, says that for Christ he has suffered the loss of everything, and counts it as rubbish, if only he is found in Christ and comes to a share in his resurrection.

But would you believe me if I said that God loves you as if you were the God of God? I think you'd find that hard to believe. I know I do. And yet, St. Thomas Aquinas, one of the greatest and most sober-minded theologians in history, said that it was so. And well he might, for at the Last Supper the Son of God himself said, "As the Father loves me, so I also love you."

I think it is only in the light of such faith in God's love that we can really appreciate the mystery of Christmas. All three of today's readings put before us the pre-history and the history of the Messiah. Let me approach them in this way: When there is a crisis in national or international affairs, we sense the need of a great leader who can really get people together, convince them of a solution, and get them to support him in carrying it out. This era's threat of a nuclear holocaust is a time of such crisis, and we pray for great and wise leaders to guide us.

But in a much larger sense, at the fall of Adam, the whole human race fell into a crisis which no ordinary human being could solve. We needed a leader who could restore the broken relationship with God, save us from our sins, and reverse the fatal plunge into death. Clearly, such a leader must have more than human powers. That is why Isaiah pleaded, "Let the heavens rain down the Just One, and the earth bring forth a Savior." It's a most profound plea, because this Savior should be human, but more than human. He should come out of the earth, as it were, as Adam did, but he also has to have divine power, that is, he has to come down from heaven.

In the revelation, beginning with the fall of Adam, God promised a leader who would come and save us. The Bible names him the Messiah, a Hebrew word which refers to the *Savior*. His power and authority to accomplish the messianic task could come only from God. That notion is contained in the very word, Messiah, which means "the anointed one," and is translated into Greek as *Christos,* and from Greek to English as Christ. So, in a popular sense, Messiah, Savior, and Christ, are all interchangeable.

Today's three readings present us with the three stages of the Messiah: In the first reading, he is still being promised; in the Gospel he is conceived in the womb of Mary; and in the reading from Paul his power goes out to save the world.

King David wanted to build God a house — that is, a Temple. God, however, tells David that, on the contrary, he, God, will build David an eternal house, in the sense of a dynasty. The Jews understood this well as meaning that the Messiah was to be a descendant of David. In today's psalm, the prophecy is repeated.

In the Gospel reading of a thousand years later the promise is fulfilled. It's a tense, dramatic, even fearful scene. A mighty, powerful archangel pulls up like a heavily armed battleship at the little wharf of Mary's home. He tells her not to be afraid. He gives her his message: God has promised David an heir. That heir is to be born of her. Joseph, her husband-to-be, who is of the line of David, will receive the promised dynasty without any action of his. Through her virginal conception of a Son, God's promise will be fulfilled. And Mary, with reverent and obedient love, yields herself to God's plan. At that moment the Incarnation takes place. Heaven and earth conceive the Messiah. The prayer of Isaiah and the whole human race has been answered.

In the second reading, written after Jesus' resurrection, Paul announces that the word of the Messiah has gone out for the world's salvation. The prophecies are in the last stages of fulfillment. But don't miss the fact that the mystery of the Messiah continues to unfold in each age and in each heart.

And don't miss the touching fact that in all three readings the Messiah is revealed in *the family*. First, there is David's family, then Mary's family, and finally there is the family of the Church, which carries him to the whole human race.

To enter more deeply into Christ, meditate on the Holy Family, with the help of the rosary. But find him also in your own family, and even bring him there, by love. We're told that from the beginning God made man and wife and their fruitfulness in God's image and likeness. Further, Christian husband and wife are joined in the marriage bond to Christ as well as one another.

Where love is, there is God; and God knows that where you have the deepest love you also have the deepest sorrows, for we all offend one another by our failures in love. In the opening prayer we prayed that we may follow Christ to resurrection through the suffering and death he endured for love.

Don't let missing love in the home deter you whether you are husband or wife, son or daughter. Where you don't find love, put love, and you will find Christ as never before.

We also find Jesus in his family the Church. Here at Mass we're immersed in his mystery and presence. In the prayer over the gifts today, this mystery is stressed in a most striking way. We will pray that the Holy Spirit, who sanctified our Mother Mary, may sanctify our gifts. We are really praying that here and now the Church may bring forth Christ in the Eucharist as Mary brought him forth in Bethlehem.

The great and hidden mystery of Jesus Christ our Savior is flashing out all around us, if we have the eyes of faith to see it, and the heart of love to embrace it.

"ABC" — Christmas, Mass at Midnight   Is 9:1-6
                                                             Tt 2:11-14
                                                             Lk 2:1-14

THE VICTORY OF CHRISTMAS

Once years ago a priest at midnight Mass told of a person who came to him to describe his suicidal impulse and even explain that he had the pills to carry it out.

Now why would a priest bring up such a sad topic on a night like this? This night we celebrate an event so great no report can do it justice, and a mystery so profound no earthly mind can ever understand it; and we're given a gift so admirable that even hearts bursting with joy could not give thanks enough.

The Child born to us on this night so long ago is the eternal God, and the Son given to us in that birth is Emmanuel, God with us. This very night he is in our midst.

Why then did the priest speak of the depressed and the suicidal on this joyous night? He did it because he was aware that the bereaved and the lonely feel doubly crushed in this season because their mood so contrasts with the joy to which the season summons all. He was aware that on Christmas there is often the clash of two claims: The birth of Christ invites all to joy and mirth, but life's harsh realities press many down. And he was aware, and we should be aware tonight, that among those listening are likely some desolate and perhaps even despairing souls.

If our hearts are full of joy, let us be doubly grateful, and not forget to pray for the broken-hearted.

But dare we proclaim joy to those in serious trouble? Would our words be mere empty sounds? For answer, let us be guided by the scriptural readings we have heard, then by human experience as a guide, and lastly by the promise of Christmas itself.

First, then, does Christ's birth call even those in grave trouble to find Christmas joy? If you heard the Gospel reading well, you are already aware that the persons involved in the first Christmas had more than their share of troubles, and yet their hearts sang at Christ's birth. The decree of a pagan ruler had uprooted Joseph and Mary, reducing them to poor unsheltered travelers when Mary was heavy with Child. And then as if without mercy and with hazard to Mary's life and her unborn Child's, nature issued its own decree: The hour of birth had come.

But that decree of nature, alarming as it was, nevertheless gave Mary her firstborn Son, and the world its eternal Savior. And lest the birth of Christ seem too much like "once upon a time," God used the decree of a pagan ruler to imprint on the calendar of history the time of his Son's entry into the world. He also used it to bring about the Child's birth not in Nazareth but in Bethlehem as the prophet had foretold.

And on that holy night a decree of God sent angels soaring with salvation's message to menial and despised shepherds. They were called not because they had something special to offer, but because they had nothing at all. And yet, perhaps they had much. Who better than poor, cold, unwashed shepherds could identify with a baby born like an outcast, sheltered in a cave and laid in a manger wrapped not in royal garments but swaddling bands?

The very heights of the Christmas mystery blend in some inexpressibly apt way with the harshness of their shepherd state. Opposites attract, and somehow it is suitable that the lowly and the homeless be first to join an incarnate God in exile from his own indescribable glory.

Do not these truths tell us that those who are crushed tonight are the most special concerns of the Christmas Lord?

Now let the evidence from our daily lives encourage us further. Does not life itself teach us that progress is preceded by struggle, that human growth is a dying and a rising, that human victories generally lie at the end of a string of many failures? Are not almost all the roads to success paved with suffering, sorrow and struggle? Did not Jesus have to travel such a road to work out our salvation?

Finally, does not the nature of Christmas itself encourage us to throw off the yoke of our griefs and win by struggle the victory of a joyous Christmas? Is it not the promise in things that orients us toward the future? Christmas is no different. Tender as is our regard for the Infant Christ, Christmas carries us not backward but forward. Christ's birth was a beginning from which he himself had to struggle forward; and his birthday is a reminder that we must go forward to the day when he will come again. With hope we look to the age when the present sorrows will exist no more, and the true promise of Christmas will arrive.

For now we must pursue the promise of Christmas. We must dig deep into its hidden content. St. John described its real meaning in those golden words, ''Herein is love, not that we loved God, but that he loved us and sent his Son.'' As Paul tells us in the second reading, God offers salvation to all, and offers all of us training in rejecting godless ways. Have we failed? Are we failing? He came to encourage us and help us begin again.

Elsewhere Paul says expressly that God saved us not for any righteous deeds we had done, but through his kindness. Let us not dare be depressed over our sins tonight. Like a pawn-shop ticket, they are our claim to our Savior.

Tonight of all nights our deeds good or bad weigh less than a featherweight in the windstorm of God's passion of outpoured love. None need feel less redeemed than anyone else if only he says, "I'm sorry. Save me, God my Savior." To refuse that trust is to make God's love meaningless. Does anyone want to argue morality and merits tonight? Let him answer this question: Were the saints living in Jerusalem called to Christ's birth that night, or only ordinary shepherds? God calls whom he pleases. Everything is a gift. God gave his Jerusalem saints their holiness, and he gave his shepherds their wondrous privilege.

If we believe in love and return love nothing else will matter much, and what we took for tragedies will be revealed as a sharing with Simon of Cyrene in the privilege of helping the Son born in Bethlehem to carry his cross to Calvary.

Over the years many lovely Christmas cards have been sent, but God sent the loveliest of all. He sent the Word made flesh. The message of his love is written in his living heart: He loves you and delivered himself for you. So when he is born in mystery in this hour from the "womb" of the altar, take hold of him as the shepherds certainly did. Take him into the home of your hands, your heart and your flesh, and rejoice that he has come.

"ABC" — Christmas, Mass During the Day   Is 52:7-10
                                                          Heb 1:1-6
                                                          Jn 1:1-18

THE FIRST CHRISTMAS PRESENT

When Malcolm Muggeridge went to India to do a film on Mother Teresa of Calcutta, he wanted pictures of the home where Mother Teresa attended the dying with such love. His professional cameraman, Ken Macmillan, insisted the place was too dark, but he tried anyway. The result was scenes "bathed in a particularly beautiful light'' which Ken insisted was technically impossible, and which Muggeridge considered a true miracle and called ''the Kindly Light'' of God, making visible the love in the room.

Whatever the truth of that matter, imagine the spiritual radiance shining round the newborn Baby in the cave at Bethlehem. How we would love to have been there!

The Christmas Masses convey us to that holy scene in several ways. At the midnight Mass, the Gospel took us with Mary and Joseph to the stable in Bethlehem, and there we saw Jesus born. And we heard the angels announcing him as Messiah and Lord to the shepherds in the fields. In the Mass at dawn we returned with the shepherds to gaze at this Child whom the Scriptures had promised and whom the angels declare the promises' fulfillment. And we heard St. Paul saying that it is not by any deeds of ours that this has happened, but by the loving kindness of our God.

And now at this Mass during the day we return to gaze with faith into the inner mystery of this Child, to see what his birth really means. We are told by St. John that ''the Word was made flesh.''

What is this ''Word''? Using that term, God is revealing to us his deep, deep mystery. Let us pause and struggle for a moment to understand. The most spiritual part of us is our mind and our will. Before we say any word, we first conceive a spiritual thought in our mind, and then only does it appear on our lips. God is telling us that this is the closest we can come to understanding what happened in eternity. The divine Father, the first person of the Blessed Trinity, begot a Son who is also a pure Spirit like himself. This whole mysterious eternal act of divine fatherhood is purely spiritual; and so, to give us some grasp of the mystery by speaking of it in words, the divine Son is called the *Word* of the Father.

It is so appropriate that we go back this way, because unless we understand something of the eternal beginnings of the Child who was born in Bethlehem, we really don't understand anything at all of the mystery.

The angels told the shepherds that this Child is the Savior, but we know more than that. So let us look now at the meaning of Christmas, at the effects of Christmas, and at the fact that Christmas goes forward much more than it goes back.

First, then, the meaning of Christmas is precisely this: that God the divine Son, who existed from all eternity in the heart of the Father, was born of the Virgin Mary and became Man. He became a human being as real as you and I. In fact, the Fathers of the Church said that he redeemed only what he took. If he had not taken our full human nature, body and soul, he would not have redeemed our full human stock. But he did take a full human nature. He became everything we are, except in the area of sin. And he did not redeem our sin; he redeemed us from sin. The Church Fathers summarize the mystery in one pithy phrase. They say that Jesus is everything that God is and everything we are. That is the meaning of Christmas.

We have recalled the Son's birth in eternity to understand his birth in time. The message of this Mass is that the Word became flesh and dwelt among us. He is born to us not just as Christ our Savior, but as God our Savior. He is Emmanuel, God-with-us. He was the Son of the Father for an eternity before he became the Son of Mary in time.

Now let us look at the effects of Christmas on us. The first effect is that God gave us his Son. The human race prayed and longed for him through the ages. He was born of Mary, but in a sense we the whole human race conceived him by our prayers. God heard us, and gave us the first Christmas present, his divine Son.

The effect of his coming is that God became easy to know. The day he was born of Mary is the day our five senses could embrace him and rejoice. This is the theological meaning of Christmas, that the Son of God became Son of man, and in doing so he has both revealed God and redeemed mankind.

Do you know what it means that he has become one of us? It means that we can come to know him by coming to know ourselves, for he now shares our human nature. He revealed himself to us by becoming like us.

Another effect of Christmas that St. John's Gospel brings out strongly is that the Child of God has become our Child to make us children of God. That is why in today's prayers we ask to share his sonship, his kingdom, his glory, and his praise of the Father. "Christian," cried Pope St. Leo the Great in a Christmas homily, "know your dignity."

Thirdly and finally, let us realize that Christianity goes forward much more than it goes back. Even if we long to go back to Mary giving birth, we must remember that Christianity always goes forward to fulfillment, even this very day, among us, the people of God.

You can make a pilgrimage to Bethlehem and see the cave where Jesus was born, and the place where Mary lay when she delivered him. It is a devout thing to do, but what we do this morning is far, far better. In Bethlehem, the Child was wrapped in swaddling clothes and laid in a manger — a place where animals eat. Today he will be wrapped in bread and laid in vessels for our food. And so we will receive in Holy Communion the Christ of Bethlehem, who rose from the dead to be our life.

His love accepts nothing less than to become one with us. Let us be as loving, accepting nothing less than to become one with him. That is why he came, and why we came here. Christmas is not just the memory of his birth, but the celebration of his birthday, the birthday of our Lord and our God. Let us receive him, adore him, and share our happiness with him and one another.

"B" — Holy Family

Si 3:2-6, 12-14
Col 3:12-21
Lk 2:22-40

GOD'S GUIDE TO FAMILY LIFE

People everywhere today are using photocopiers. They're great when they work, but when they don't the prime rule is,

"Refer to the Instruction Book." Manufacturers know their products and know how to guide us in their use. Similarly, when we're having family problems, should we not refer to the instructions of God the Maker and Creator of family life?

In this holy season the Son of God was born a man of the Virgin Mary on the first Christmas. Today we turn our gaze on his human family. By gazing on the Holy Family of Nazareth we see better how we should live life in our own families.

Someone has said that the trouble with family life is that it is so *daily*, and that Santa Claus has it easy: He visits families only once a year. To show love every day is not easy. Yet the Holy Family did it, and we can do it, too.

Today the Lord puts forward his guidelines for family life in the scriptural word read to us. Some reject them, some are enchanted by them, and some are half-hearted toward them. One of the reasons for the failure to listen is that secular society promotes norms opposed to God's, whether to win votes or lower government expenses. And of course the result is that many families fail to survive.

We are invited in this hour to reflect in faith on family life as it is guided by God. We picture the Child Jesus living with Mary and Joseph in the Holy Family.

Pope Paul VI, on a visit to Nazareth, made a beautiful reflection on what the Holy Family teaches us. We don't have to go there on our feet, and look at the shrine of the little home where Mary dwelt; we don't have to walk down the street to the building where her boyfriend, Joseph, lived, and then the Holy Family together. But we do have to go there in mind and heart if we want to pattern our families after the model God has given us.

On the wall of that shrine is a well-known image of the Boy Jesus at work in the carpenter shop with his foster-father, Joseph. That is where we go in spirit now as we reflect on this holy and very human mystery. That family probably lived more poorly and primitively, in accord with the times, than any family here today.

They had their struggles. We hear in today's Gospel how they took the Baby from Bethlehem to the Temple in nearby Jerusalem. For sacrifice they didn't offer anything expensive like a lamb; they offered a couple of pigeons. St. Luke is telling us delicately that they were making the offering of a poor family.

They struggled like every poor family. Before ever they got back to Nazareth from the Child's birth in Bethlehem, they had to rush into exile in Egypt to save his life. They were poor aliens in a foreign land, and probably did not even know the language. Just how long they had to stay we don't know, but at last they were able to return to their little hill town in Galilee.

And no doubt they had their human struggles in getting along together, because it's not always easy even if we love deeply. One English writer wrote the bitter statement, "We kill the things we love." How many families have begun by loving one another very much and ended by killing their love with selfishness, criticism, ranting and raving, and finally, hatred?

The Holy Family never let that happen, but they had to struggle to grow in love. Even Jesus had to learn to grow in love for he lived a human life. Their life is a real guide for us because it is as real as our own. This God-given guide is not a dream but a reality we can imitate.

Picture Joseph coming home from work late, with Mary trying to keep the food hot. What did she say? Picture Joseph coming home hungry and finding some food on the table that he had never cared for. Did he say anything? Picture the Boy Jesus trying to do his studies, and being told to get up and do this or that. Did he delay? Did he complain? Or did he do it? Our hearts will give us the answers, and they will be answers for our own lives. They will bring happiness to our families and even make us saints.

Can we imagine Jesus, Mary or Joseph rejecting any of the guidelines for family life God gives us in that first reading from the book of Sirach? Did you notice how realistic it is? It doesn't say we should obey our parents because they're perfect. It's so realistic it says that even if your father starts losing his mind in his old age, still be considerate. As we grow up we know our parents aren't perfect, but they are still in God's place in our lives, for they gave us life.

Wise people keep looking for a way to guide their conduct by a few brief rules. Well, here's one set for family life: Wives, always ask yourselves the question: What would Mary do? Husbands, ask yourselves: What would Joseph do? Children, ask yourselves: What would the Child Jesus do? Then do it. And let's all make it our Prayer of the Week to say daily, "Jesus, Mary and Joseph, make my family a holy family too." And also be aware that every time you receive Holy Communion you become all the more a bond of love in your family because the Eucharist is the greatest of all bonds of love.

Finally, here are *A Baker's Dozen for Spouses* to which I think Mary and Joseph would say Amen!

1) Be generous to the desires of your partner.
2) Criticize rarely and with love.
3) If you must neglect someone never let it be him/her.
4) Make your mate shine.
5) A compliment-a-day is more important than a vitamin-a-day.
6) Meet like Adam and Eve for the first time, with a sign of affection.
7) Never both be angry.
8) When you're wrong say you're sorry and settle before sundown.
9) Never, never throw up past mistakes.
10) Pray together and be aware of your oneness in Christ.
11) Never ask (or give) what God forbids.
12) It takes two to quarrel. Subtract one.
13) Don't yell unless the house is burning down!

"ABC" — Epiphany

Is 60:1-6
Ep 3:2-3, 5-6
Mt 2:1-12

CALLED BY LIGHT DIVINE

Are you aware that the Gospels don't tell us the day or even the month in which Christ was born? The Church had to set a date on which to celebrate Christmas. Before doing so, it set a date to celebrate this feast of the Epiphany. It is one of the most important feasts in the calendar year, especially in the early Church for those Christians who were not born Jews. The word *Epiphany* means manifestation or disclosure. It is the day on which the Savior was disclosed to the non-Jewish world, represented by the three astrologers. On this day faith in Christ began to become world-wide.

Each day we walk by three different lights: the light of the eye, the light of the mind, and the light of faith. The light of faith is God himself. His light shines on us through his self-revelation in prophecies and in his own divine Son. Faith is the "eye" by which we see this divine light. On the Epiphany the light of revelation shone out from the newborn Christ and the first non-Jews saw it with the eye of faith and worshipped.

In the first reading we have an astonishing prophecy about that light divine. Ages ago the prophet Isaiah told the tiny Jewish nation — the nation of faith — that in a future time the nations would come pouring in, led by the light of God.

The prophecy is particularly astonishing because it is continually being proved true. The astrologers began the fulfillment. We Christians, a billion strong, continue it today around the world.

Let us reflect on the fact that the astrologers came as faith-bearers, that we are appointed faith-bearers, and that union with Christ is the torch of our faith.

First, the astrologers came as faith-bearers. By the eye of faith they followed the light of the star and the light of the prophet Micah and came to the light of Christ.

They came by the eye of faith, but they found among the chosen people of faith many who had gone blind. It's clear Herod had no true faith. He had superstition enough to fear some schemer was being born who might usurp his kingly reign.

But let us not be too hard on the Chosen People lest we condemn ourselves. Many unbelievers around us remain unbelieving because to them our faith, too, looks dead. Mahatma Gandhi took his doctrine of pacifism from the Sermon on the Mount. He said he would have become a Christian if he had seen Christians living what Jesus taught. The Nihilist Society of this country ran an ad which said, "Isn't it pretty silly to keep invoking the idea of God when it's pretty obvious no one takes him seriously as anything but a ten-point question on a theology exam?"

Would they have to change their minds if they examined into your life? One priest asked an acquaintance, "How is your new job going?" The man replied, "I had to be dishonest, so I quit." The Nihilists would have to take that Christian's faith seriously.

Today, we have an experience that should give us a more merciful view of the Jews of Jesus' time. They were afraid of going astray. So are many of us today in this time of a faith-crisis in the Church. Cardinal Ratzinger, who heads the Congregation for the Doctrine of the Faith, has powerfully described the crisis, and the Holy Father has spoken and acted to reduce it. The Church has had to disown more than one theologian who is misleading the faithful. At the time of Jesus there had been a false messiah, so people then were worried and it made it that much more difficult to recognize Christ when he came.

Our faith is sound if it holds to Christ our Light in accord with the teaching of his Church. Christ founded his Church to bring the whole human race to share in his redemptive work.

Secondly, we are called to be faith-bearers. Our faith may be sound, but it is mature only if we are at work to share it with others.

The Second Vatican Council stressed this in its Decree on the Apostolate of the Laity. It said that you laity too share in the priestly, prophetic, and kingly office of Christ. It said *Christ himself* appoints you to be apostles of his mission in the world. Genuine love for Christ and for all others impels you to share salvation with all you can reach.

The Council called us to follow the example of our Blessed Mother by helping one another in every kind of necessity. It referred to work with families, and of course your first job is to see that Christ lives among you in your own family; but it also listed the following activities: adopt orphans, welcome strangers, help to run the schools, teach catechism, give teenagers advice and help, and assist engaged couples to make a better preparation for marriage (11). I would add that any couple which uses Natural Family Planning should make a special effort to engage in the work of spreading it because they will have learned what a tremendous blessing it is.

The Council spoke of the work of the Catholic laity in civic affairs. As patriots and citizens in the world, they ought to use their citizenship and political rights to promote the true common good. By working for just and merciful laws and legislation to provide jobs for all, they improve their country and prepare the way for the Gospel. In that context, how can we forget the silent scream of the unborn? The Council indicated that the work of the laity is so central to the Church that training for it should start with a child's earliest education and be intensified among teenagers. Christ has shared his kingdom with each of us. St. Ignatius of Loyola put it this way: "What have I done for Christ? What am I doing for Christ? What do I intend to do for Christ?"

Thirdly, union with Christ is the torch of our faith. On this feast of the Epiphany of Christ, we should realize that the soul of the apostolate is Christ. If we don't have him, how can we give him to anybody? We have to keep going deeper into his Sacred Heart by prayer and worship. Today's Mass helps us. In the Prayer over the

Gifts, we recall the astrologers' gifts to Christ and ask God to receive our gift, which is Christ himself. In the Post-Communion Prayer, we beg to truly recognize Christ in the Eucharist and give him a welcome of love. When Christ becomes our very heart and our love bursts with the need to share him with others we ourselves become an epiphany, a disclosure of Christ to the world. And that's what we pray to be today.

"B" — Baptism of the Lord   Is 42:1-4, 6-7
                                                           Ac 10:34-38
                                                           Mk 1:7-11

SON, SERVANT AND MESSIAH

We've gone through the mysteries of the infancy of Jesus and suddenly today he comes to us as a man at his baptism and the beginning of his public life. But we should see today's event as a continuation of the epiphany, that is, the revelation of Jesus' identity. First his birth revealed him to Mary and Joseph, then an angel revealed him to the shepherds and a star revealed him to the wise men. Now the Holy Trinity reveals him to his people and to us.

It should provoke us to deep thought that Jesus continues to be revealed to us in the midst of family. At his birth he is found in his Holy Family; as he comes to us at his baptism he is identified with his Divine Family, the Family that is God the Holy Trinity. And in the course of history, he is found in his family, the Church.

Let's pause here to reflect on family. If we sat and discussed the meaning and import of family life we might agree that family life has its problems and at times can be very difficult, but there is no substitute. Family is the center of our lives, and by God's plan it is also the source of our lives. And for those who become parents, it is the center out of which to give life. So family, by the plan of God, is central to all human life. That realization is, I think, intended by the mysteries we are celebrating.

Today's readings lead us to ponder the following truths: that at Jesus' baptism the "First Family" became manifest; that Jesus called us to share in the mystery of his baptism; and finally, that Jesus was anointed by the Spirit to bring the kingdom, and so were we at our baptism.

First, then, at Jesus' baptism we are introduced to the "First Family," the family of God, the divine Trinity. This is a solemn moment, rare even in the Bible. Is there ever again a time when the three persons of the Holy Trinity manifest themselves so clearly as at Jesus' baptism?

Jesus has just left his human family to begin his public life. Despite his divine dignity he undergoes the humble process of baptism. And as he does, the Holy Spirit comes down in love to rest on him and identify him as the Messiah. And the divine Father addresses Jesus, publicly confesses Jesus his beloved Son, tells Jesus how pleased he is with the first thirty years of his human life, and assures Jesus he will be with him in his public life.

This is a profound and marvelous religious experience for Jesus in his human nature. If mystics like St. Catherine of Siena, St. Teresa of Avila and St. John of the Cross can tell us of the ecstasies of their private mystical experiences of God, how much more exalting was this experience for Jesus? And we, too, if we enter into the habit of prayer at the depth proper to the Christian life, will taste the graces of God's love for us and support of us.

The baptism of Jesus is a profound mystery. We struggle to grasp its meaning. Baptism is a washing away of sin. Jesus had no sin, so why be baptized? Isaiah the prophet sheds light on the answer. In foretelling the Messiah, Isaiah said he would suffer for the sins of others. And St. Paul says in a shattering phrase that Jesus was "made sin" for us. Through our baptism into him he became identified with us and therefore with our sins. And so he had to wash them away. St. Gregory Nazianzus says that Jesus was baptized to wash the waters with his body so they could wash away our sins through baptism and the Holy Spirit. These are the depths of this great mystery in which we participate this morning.

Isaiah tells us in the first reading how kind and tender this Spirit-anointed Messiah will be. He will treat sin-loaded people with "kid gloves" so they won't fall into despair. Let that remind us of Jesus' own words, "Learn of me, for I am meek and humble of heart."

The Father identifies Jesus as his Son, but Isaiah prophesied that he would be "the servant of God." Jesus is both Son and Servant. We can find the explanation in Jesus' parable of the father who told his two sons to go out and work in the vineyard. One went and the other didn't. The one who went deserved the name of son and servant and the one who refused deserved neither name. For if we are not willing to serve our parents, who were servants to us in our childhood, we don't deserve to be called son or daughter. It's a name we not only receive, but have to earn. Jesus is Son and Servant of the Father, but not only of the Father; he served us as well. All of this is contained or implied in this mystery of Jesus' baptism.

Secondly, Jesus had us baptized into him and his Divine Family. By our baptism we were reborn in Christ as children of God. Christ is our life. That is the depth of the Christian mystery.

The Church is the bride of Christ and we are her children born from her baptismal womb. If our natural family is so important that without it we could not be born, see how important the Church is to our birth into eternal life! We belong to the family of the Church by the necessary gift of God. We put up with the faults of our family the Church as we put up with those in our natural family. Both families are composed of sinners like ourselves.

There is another touching aspect to the baptism of Jesus. A young man who falls in love with a girl and hopes to marry her introduces her to his family. His family will become hers as well. And so here we find Jesus introducing his bride, the Church, to his Family, the Holy Trinity.

Finally then: As at his baptism, Jesus was anointed by the Spirit to go forth and pray and labor and suffer even to death to bring the kingdom of God, so were we at ours. We share in the life, the labors and the way of life of Jesus. Some people seem to shy away as if they can't imitate Jesus. It's sinful to think that. If the Christmas mystery teaches us anything, it is that Jesus was really human by his birth from Mary. The imitation of Christ is our calling.

We know how Jesus lived. In the second reading Peter tells us with childlike simplicity that Jesus "went about doing good works." That's our calling too. He prayed and worked and put up with the sins and the failings and the rejection of his people. We must too.

In the opening prayer we asked our heavenly Father to keep us faithful to our baptismal calling. We have to use the grace we ask. Too many have the attitude, "Oh, I can't really become holy." But in fact we can. A woman once asked the great theologian, St. Thomas Aquinas, "How can I be saved?" He said, "By willing it." That's how we can become holy: by willing it. Everything else is in place. God never fails in his graces. Will to be holy, and live what you will.

Jesus, at his baptism, began to share with us even his Divine Family and Mary his mother. Made like him in baptism, let us share with him and his, especially our own family, all we have and are.

"B" — Second Sunday of the Year   1 S 3:3-10, 19
1 Cor 6:13-15, 17-20
Jn 1:35-42

CALLING THE JOHNS AND ANDREWS STILL

God has given us family life so that we may live in a community of love and be led back to God and eternal life. But some men and women don't want to wait for eternity. Hearing a call in their hearts, they leave everything now and follow Jesus as the first disciples did.

The special call certain men and women in the Gospel had to walk personally with Jesus during his time on earth has always fascinated the Christian people. The desire to do likewise has never faded from our ranks. This special call from Christ we have named *Vocation*. It is a call to sacrifice private family life to serve the whole family of God as a priest, Sister or Brother.

The one called will find his family either hostile or supportive. One young boy wrote a priest about his desire to be a priest. After they corresponded for a while the boy wrote a shocked letter. "I told my father I wanted to be a priest," he said, "and you'd think I'd murdered someone." Soon he stopped writing. Many parents, though, are supportive. One mother, hearing her son confide his intention of becoming a priest, said, "Now I feel my life is worthwhile."

Today's Gospel records the call of the first disciples, Andrew and John. The readings also record Jesus' own vocation. In the Psalm are the words, "Behold I come. In the written scroll it is prescribed for me. To do your will, O my God, is my delight." That was Jesus' own call. What was the Father's will for him? John the Baptist tells us when he says of Jesus, "There is the Lamb of God." Jesus was called to be the true Lamb of Sacrifice for the sins of the world.

At those words of the Baptist, John and Andrew followed Jesus and he asked them what they wanted. They wanted him, the Savior. They wanted to join him, live with him and share his work for the world's salvation. That is the heart of religious vocation. But notice their answer: They didn't presume to say, "We want you!" They felt in their hearts that *he* had to invite and call them; so they said, "Rabbi, where do you stay?" And to their eternal joy he said, "Come and see."

In most cases the call doesn't begin so clearly. Often a boy feels called to the priesthood, but doesn't feel worthy, so he says nothing. And usually he has other, conflicting interests, so a battle goes on in his heart. He studies, he dates, he looks for the girl who will share his life. He thinks of different careers that interest him. He thinks of his future, of death and eternal life. And perhaps after a devout Holy Communion the call of vocation flares up, and he wavers back and forth. If he prays, his vocation grows stronger. He feels that if eternal life with God is the deepest meaning of life, he must bypass all else and start there. He must become a priest! And so he talks to a priest at last, and enters the seminary.

And if he has a call, he finds joy. One seminarian stayed for a while in a house of priests before he went off to study theology. When he left for his studies, he posted a note saying, "Thank you for your kindness. I've been inspired by your life of faith. It has been a slice of heaven being here." So must Andrew and John have felt.

Jesus made the priesthood necessary to the Church. Pope John Paul II said, "Without the Eucharist there is no Church. And without the priest there is no Eucharist." Jesus chooses men to stand in his person in the Church, teaching, sanctifying, and governing. Through baptism he gave all of us a share in his priesthood, but through ordination he gives the priest alone the power to speak his words at the consecration, while he stands by to bring about what the words convey. And so with the other sacraments.

The sacrament of Holy Orders has three grades. Only the bishop is ordained to the fullness of the priesthood. The other priests are his helpers, and deacons help both. All are servants of the people of God, in the likeness of Christ, who came to serve.

Canon 1029 lists the qualities a man needs to be ordained. He must have an integral faith, right intention, the required knowledge, a good reputation, good morals, proven virtue, and other necessary physical and psychological qualities. If his call is genuine, God and the Church confer on him the sacrament of the priesthood.

When a man asks to enter the seminary, Church leaders make a judgment over a period of years as to whether he is called. As late as the Ordination ceremony the people present, who know him well, are asked if he is worthy to be ordained. It is no empty question. His call is from God, but his acceptance is from the people. Even with their approval, his pastoral role is no easy task.

Let's be grateful to God for the priestly gift, and thankful to those who give their life to it. We all need priests; even priests need priests. When I want to receive the sacrament of reconciliation, to whom can I go but another priest? When I'm sick, and long for Holy Communion, who can consecrate it but another priest? When I fall gravely ill, who can anoint me but a brother priest?

We take as a model of love and reverence for priests the Blessed Virgin Mary. When Christ the great High Priest hung on the cross offering his sacrifice, she stood lovingly at his feet joining his offering, and offering herself with him. When St. John offered Holy Mass, she was present, so grateful that Christ had chosen him to make the Holy Sacrifice present once again, and to give her the Bread of Angels whom she had conceived in her womb. Priests take Mary as their mother who gives them loving care and confirming support.

We priests need our people's support, especially now that the faith and morals we must teach are received so hostilely by the world, and by those Christians who have absorbed too much of the world. Remember that our teaching is not ours, but his who sent us.

Pray always for priestly and religious vocations. There is a crisis in the Church. The lack of vocations is both a part of and a result of that crisis. Remember the little boy I mentioned above, and be aware that the example and the attitudes, the faith and the morals in the home support or undermine vocation.

If we value Christ our Savior, let us esteem the priest Christ himself chooses to stand in his place; if we value Holy Communion, let us value those chosen to consecrate it so that we may be fed.

Don't expect too much of priests. They are human beings like you. An atheist once told a priest he would believe when he met a priest who neither ate nor went to the bathroom. The priest said, ''You don't want a priest; you want an angel.'' The priest is given the grace necessary to his calling, but must serve others holier than himself. God gives his greatest graces to whom he pleases.

God continues to call the Johns and Andrews. Let us pray they will hear and respond for love of Christ and the whole people of God.

"B" — Third Sunday of the Year

Jon 3:1-5, 10
1 Cor 7:29-31
Mk 1:14-20

SAINTS AND LOST IDENTITIES

There was a kingdom where civil war raged with all its dangers. The king sent his two infant children in the care of a guardian to a foreign land. There the guardian died suddenly. The children were left without identity — orphans who did not know they were a prince and princess with claim to a kingdom.

The parable represents this world where the civil war of sin rages on. Sin's darkness has so invaded the human mind that many don't know who they are or where they came from. All who do not regain their identity by faith remain anonymous orphans of the universe. Our faith identifies us as adopted sons and daughters of God called to be saints. The readings today are about this call to recover our identity and pass from sin to sainthood.

What then is a saint? The first class of saints are all who are in heaven with God. Some of them have been recognized by the Church as saints, and canonized, but most have been recognized only by God. There will never be a non-saint in heaven. The second class of saints, as St. Paul makes clear, includes all of us who by faith are living our call to become saints.

Are we grateful to God that faith has given us our true identity? Some people come to it tragically late. One man lying in a coma suddenly sat bolt upright and cried, "I've done it all wrong. I've done it all wrong!" He fell back into the coma and died. Another man who was dying said to a priest, "Now I know the only thing that counts is God." On one's deathbed that shouldn't be hard to see. Aren't we blessed if we see it now? And see that the only tragedy is not to become a saint?

Today's readings invite us to reflect along three lines. First, Christ is calling us to recover fully our identity. Secondly, he calls us to live it. Thirdly, he calls us to help others, especially the young, to live their call to noble living.

First, Christ is calling us to recover fully our identity. To do it we have to reform. The word as Jesus used it means to have a change of mind and heart about values. The world has its values upside down. We have to turn them right side up and recognize that sin is endless grief and not the shrewdness the world pretends it to be. It is incurably evil. We come to this new value system by accepting the Good News that Christ is our Savior, our Lord, our God and our life, and that his teaching is our way. In him we learn our identity as children of God given us by our Creator. All other values must be put in their place relative to God. If necessary they must all be sacrificed as the martyrs sacrificed them.

Secondly, we are called to live according to this conversion. That's what Paul is telling us in the second reading. It's difficult both to understand, and to live. Yet it's easy if we are faithful to God's grace. It's difficult to understand Paul when he says you must live as though you're not married even though you are, and you must weep as if you weren't weeping, and conduct your business as though you didn't have one.

Is he saying, "Live apart from your spouse"? Of course not. God says, "What God has joined together let no man put asunder." Is he saying, "Don't love your spouse"? Of course not. He says the opposite elsewhere. He is simply telling us to make nothing God, except God. Don't make a God of your spouse or your business or your sorrows. Don't make a God of the world. Don't make an eternity of time. It's important to see the folly of all that now as we'll see it on our deathbed, or at least at our judgment.

Once we see the relativity and the relative value of all things but God, we will be free to live the truth which Christ is teaching us in our hearts this very hour.

Thirdly and finally we're called to help others, especially the young, to follow their aspirations to noble deeds. The great philosopher Aristotle described the young very well. "They are hot tempered and quick-tempered," he said, "and apt to give way to their anger . . . For owing to their love of honor they cannot bear being slighted and are indignant if they imagine themselves unfairly treated. While they love honor they love victory more. For youth is eager for superiority over others . . . They love both more than they love money, which indeed they love very little, not having learned yet what it means to be without it."

Aristotle recognized that the young aspire to noble deeds. The Christian explanation is that the young have the advantage of having sprung fresh from the creative word of God. They haven't yet lost what he told them of the innocence and the holiness of love.

It calls them to heroic dedication, self-mastery, and self-giving. Fresh from the Creator, they're homesick for holiness.

Our Lord knew that when he called the young men in today's Gospel to leave everything and follow him. And they did. We too should support the high aspirations of youth.

One father had a son he loved very much. When the boy reached his twenties he began to take up with a religious cult that invited him to go after riches as God's gift. His father was disgusted, but didn't recognize that by not adhering to a faith himself he had left a vacuum in his son's life. And a religion with distorted values was sucked into that vacuum.

That is a tragedy you can avoid. Love God above all and love and serve your family in him, and your holiness will be contagious. That's what sanctity is. That's what it is to be a saint. Alan Ameche, the football star, had a son of twenty-two who died in an auto accident. At the end of the funeral Mass, Alan stood up and said, "Don't be afraid to love your children while you still have time." He told how happy he was for the times he hadn't been afraid to give his son an embrace and a kiss while he still had the chance. Let us show Christlike love while we have time. Or too late we'll find that life is short and eternity is long. We will be, or miss being, saints forever.

I can't finish this homily. You have to do it. Accept the identity Christ bestows on you. Say to yourself now, "I'm called to be a saint." You might feel like laughing at the idea as Sarah laughed when told she was going to become a mother in her old age. But she did become a mother. And we will either become saints or eternal tragedies. So say now, in the quiet of your heart before we begin the Creed, "I understand, Lord. I'm called to become a saint."

Dt 18:15-20
1 Cor 7:32-35
Mk 1:21-28

OUR POWER FOR PURITY

In a powerful act of authority, Jesus casts out an unclean spirit. How we need that power for purity in today's culture! The world is staggered by a crisis of sexual immorality and sexual diseases. God has given us marriage as the only valid sexual union, but the world rejects that teaching. Not only is there widespread premarital sex and homosexual practices, but so many couples are living out of wedlock that ours has been called The Post-marital Society. The immorality crisis invaded first the Protestant Churches and then the Catholic Church. Lutheran Pastor Richard John Neuhaus has called on the Roman Catholic Church to be the lead Church in revitalizing Christianity.

The Church has God's authority to teach his law of sexual purity, and teaches it. It teaches that all sexual activity outside of marriage is wrong. It teaches that masturbation, homosexual activity, premarital sex, adultery, impure thoughts and desires, and the pornographic books, films and TV programs are immoral and seriously sinful. In marriage itself, the goodness, holiness and wholesomeness of the marriage act must be cherished and guarded. The only honest form of family planning is Natural Family Planning. The Church teaches it worldwide.

How grateful I am that when I was young the Church clearly and strongly taught me God's law. Nothing else could have given me the strength to struggle for purity. Now it is our turn to teach by word and conduct the young among us.

Some people think they can ignore this authoritative teaching without consequences, but they are wrong. God has appointed nature itself to be a corrective. ''Nature is God's vicar general,'' says Medical Doctor Herbert Ratner. ''If you don't listen to nature, if you ignore her," he says, "she hits right back at you." He suggests that the epidemic of venereal diseases and AIDS is nature's way of showing that God's law is being broken. Ages ago St. Augustine said that every sin carries its own punishment, which God allows but does not will positively. We all know that alcoholism can kill, and drugs can kill. So too can promiscuous sex. It can kill bodies and souls and marriages. Many people thought that premarital sex in "trial marriages" would make for better marriages. Researchers of that conviction did a survey and were shocked to learn that those who lived together before they married were more likely to divorce than those who had not. God's law is always for our good.

Some who weren't listening to God are listening to his Vicar General. One man said that as a result of the AIDS crisis, "I discovered purity." And the film industry, hard hit by the AIDS crisis, began reworking some of its films. In one, the heroine works her way out of promiscuous conduct.

Now we will look at our call to purity guided by today's readings. First, Christ the New Moses has come with the perfect law of chastity. Second, God gives us the strength and joy to live his law. Third, the Eucharist assures us victory.

First, Christ the new Moses has come with the new law of chastity. In the first reading, Moses promised that God would send a new Moses. This was a promise of Christ the Messiah. In today's Gospel the Messiah has come and is at work casting out an unclean spirit. He is showing his power and authority to cast out impurity. He passed on his authority to Peter and his successor, the Holy Father; and he gave his Church the sacraments which give each of us power to cast impurity out of our lives.

Preferring to follow the world, many turn a deaf ear to Christ teaching through his Church. They decide to make up their own minds. John Henry Cardinal Newman can illuminate us here. He was an Anglican who studied the whole history of Christianity to prove the Catholic Church wrong and the Anglican Church right.

His study taught him the opposite. He learned that where St. Peter's successor the Holy Father had been listened to, the purity of the Gospel was preserved. He came to realize that while we have to follow our consciences, we have to form our consciences by the Holy Father. So he converted to the Church.

In the second reading St. Paul goes beyond purity in marriage. He invites any who feel called to give up marriage altogether for love of God. Christ himself gave that call, as you know. The world is so blind in its worship of sex that it thinks those who don't marry either hate marriage or are unnatural. But if a person spends what money he has to buy a house and not a car, is it because he hates cars or because he prefers houses? Similarly, Christians who give up marriage do it not because they don't long for marriage but because they long more for God. They begin to live in an imperfect way here on earth the life of union with God that we'll all live in heaven. In heaven, Jesus taught, "they are neither married nor given in marriage, but live like the angels." So Christ calls us to be pure in the use of sex, or even to begin now to live like the angels for love of God.

Secondly, God gives us the strength and joy to live his law of purity. To live sexually pure is not easy. Even holy King David fell into adultery. By his sin he learned, as he says in the Psalms, that we can't keep pure by our own powers but only by the grace of God. It's a grace to pray and struggle for and really want. St. Paul helps us want it by telling us that the impure cannot enter the Kingdom of God; and that our bodies are not for immorality but for the Lord, and the Lord is for our bodies. We keep chaste for his sake, as the ever Virgin Mary did. She will help all her children to live chastely in marriage or in the single state, if only we ask her.

Thirdly, the Eucharist assures us victory. It was in a synagogue in Capernaum that Jesus cast out the unclean spirit; and it was there that he later promised to give the Eucharist. Doesn't it seem he's saying, "I cast out impure spirits; and now I'm coming to live with you to keep them out"? St. Augustine said that "one who devoutly hears Holy Mass will not fall into mortal sin, and his venial sins will be forgiven.''

Christ is God, and God can do whatever he pleases, and he is pleased to keep us pure. Once, on the Sea of Galilee, he made the roaring winds and the waves lie down like puppy dogs at his feet. He can do the same with our unruly passions. But we must want to be faithful to him, and want the gift enough to struggle and pray for it. Let's do that today as always.

''B'' — Fifth Sunday of the Year   Jb 7:1-4, 6-7
                                                            1 Cor 9:16-19, 22-23
                                                                    Mk 1:29-39

THE SACRAMENT THAT HEALS

A loving grandfather, disturbed by what he read in a spiritual book, said to a priest, "Is it true that if my little grandson Nickie gets seriously ill he can't receive the Sacrament of the Sick because he hasn't reached the age of reason?" Today's readings invite us to think about the Sacrament of the Sick, and I'll return to the priest's answer as we do so.

Job tells us in the first reading that his assignment is to suffer. Jesus told us that his assignment from the Father is to give life and give it abundantly. In today's Gospel we see him doing that by healing the sick. St. Paul's assignment is to continue the work of Christ. That is the Church's work as well, and one of its helps is the Sacrament of the Sick.

How did the Sacrament of the Sick originate? What does it do for a sick person? Who should receive it and when?

First, how did the Sacrament of the Sick originate? We hear throughout the Gospel how Jesus cured people of various diseases.

He healed them in spirit, soul and body. When sending out the Twelve to preach, he ordered them to anoint the sick and cure them. Later, when St. James wrote his letter, he said, "Is anyone among you sick? He should summon the presbyters of the Church, and they should pray over him and anoint him with oil in the name of the Lord; and the prayer of faith will save the sick person and the Lord will raise him up." So the Sacrament of Healing was instituted by Jesus, as were all the sacraments. To this day his disciples preach and forgive and cure.

Secondly, what does the Sacrament do for sick persons? Well, what do they need? When we're sick don't we feel helpless and alone? Don't we easily feel that God has abandoned us and turned against us for our sins? The sacrament meets these needs. It gives us the grace of the Holy Spirit to bolster our confidence in God and strengthen us against temptation; it helps us bear our suffering patiently and seek to overcome it. It may also heal our bodies when it is for the good of our eternal salvation.

It is God's plan that we always fight strenuously for health but sometimes, like Job in the first reading, we have from God an "assignment" to suffer. We can't know with certainty whether we suffer for our own sins or those of others. In either case, we become companions of Christ hanging on the cross doing the work of redemption. The anointing gives us the grace to bear it patiently and even sweetly with Jesus as Christians have done through the centuries.

This sacrament gives us whatever graces we need if we open our hearts to God's purposes. We're told that, when Jesus returned to his native town, "He was not able to perform any mighty deeds there" because people put no faith in him. The priest is the minister of the Sacrament of the Sick. At times he meets with that same lack of faith. If God didn't want to heal us, would he have given us this sacrament of his healing mercy?

Thirdly, who should receive this sacrament, and when, and who ought to see that they do? Canon Law explains that all the faithful who have reached the age of reason should receive it when they begin to fall seriously ill. Note that we shouldn't wait until we're near death. As a priest who has seen this sacrament at work, I will certainly ask it for myself. It's a healing sacrament, and we can best cooperate with it while we're still conscious and can open our hearts to it in faith. Also, it should be preceded by Confession and Communion so we can get the power of all three sacraments. If that is not possible, the Sacrament of the Sick has power to forgive our sins.

Note also that, in answer to the loving grandfather, Canon Law says that only those who have reached the age of reason are to receive the sacrament. Why? Because the child has been cleansed of sin by baptism. Until the age of reason he can't sin, so he has no need of a sacrament that heals by removing sin. But, as the priest explained to that grandfather, Canon Law says that if there's any likelihood the child has the use of his reason, he not only may, but should be anointed. The age of seven is generally taken as the age of reason, but that's only a rule of thumb. Tell your little children that when we get seriously sick, Jesus sends his priest to anoint us so we'll get better. Do this repeatedly until they understand. Then if they fall ill a priest may anoint them even if they haven't reached the age of seven.

People suffering infirmities of old age can be anointed even when not seriously ill. The sacrament may strengthen them bodily. It will in any case help them to bear their lot and dispose them to go home to the Father in peace when the call comes.

We all share responsibility to see that a priest visits the seriously ill. If you fall sick, ask for a priest. If a family member is the sick one, summon a priest for him. If you are in the medical profession, you too have a role to play in suggesting a priest be called, or in contacting a priest directly and asking that he drop in because the family is neglecting their duty. Medical people are very helpful because they understand better than others how much spiritual healing aids all healing.

Pray with the sick and pray over the sick yourselves. The grace of healing is not confined to a sacrament. Put a Bible at the bedside of your sick ones. Pick it up and read a passage or two to them. Remind them of God's love for them in the past.

One day we'll all come to that moment when we need to be strengthened by anointing for the final journey to the Lord. He will be waiting for us with open arms to share his eternal life with us. Whenever in the Hail Mary you ask our Blessed Mother to "pray for us now and at the hour of our death," ask her to see that at that hour you are blessed with this sacrament.

Pope Paul VI said of the Sacrament of the Sick, "Here, as in the other sacraments, the Church's main concern is of course the soul, pardon of sin and the increase of God's grace. But also, to the extent that it is up to the Church, its desire and intent is to obtain relief and if possible even healing for the sick." Here, clearly, is the mind of the Church expressed by a Pope. So we should desire this sacrament when we or our loved ones need it.

Now we turn to the Eucharist. The same Jesus who touched and healed people in today's Gospel will touch us in the Eucharist. He will give us grace for body and soul, and store up the grace that, when we need this sacrament, we may look to it eagerly.

"B" — Sixth Sunday of the Year   Lv 13:1-2, 44-46
                                                   1 Cor 10:31-11:1
                                                   Mk 1:40-45

OTHER CHRISTS AND OTHER LEPERS

We're often told we're called to be other Christs, but perhaps not warned often enough that sin lures us to become other lepers. Leprosy is the symbol of sin, but Christ, the likeness of God, heals lepers. In the Sacrament of Reconciliation Jesus heals the leprosy of sin to make us likenesses of himself.

Leprosy is the symbol of sin, but Christ is the likeness of God. The dictionary tells us leprosy is a disease that causes one to waste away and become deformed and mutilated, but that the word also means a morally or spiritually harmful influence. Thus our language itself describes leprosy as a symbol of sin.

If the moral leprosy of sin were as plain on our faces as the deformities of a leper, how differently we would behave! And how quick we'd be to seek forgiveness of our sins! If we have a good conscience we do see our moral defacement as clearly as a leper sees his pitiable state in a mirror. But when the mirror of conscience grows dull by endless sin, the sinner becomes like a leper blinded by his disease who no longer sees how he looks.

St. Paul says that God "has shone in our hearts, that we in turn might make known the glory of God shining on the face of Christ." We make the glory of God known by our imitation of Christ, which gradually transfigures us into his likeness.

Jesus heals lepers. People dreaded lepers. Their disease is contagious. The first reading tells us that if a person was found to have leprosy, he was forbidden all contact with uninfected people. In modern terminology, he was put in quarantine, as we still quarantine people with very infectious diseases.

We should admire the shrewdness of the leper in today's Gospel. He sized Jesus up as a man of God with the power to heal and the compassion to use it. He believed; he asked; he was cured. But notice something else: Instead of being grateful, he was disobedient. Though told to go quietly to the priests, he broadcast his healing abroad. The result was that Jesus had to live like a leper, in out-of-the-way places, so as not to be mobbed by cure seekers instead of seekers of the kingdom of God.

In the Sacrament of Reconciliation, Jesus heals the leprosy of sin to make us likenesses of himself. It is a great sacrament! If there were a sacrament to heal cancer or AIDS, people would flock to it day and night. This sacrament of healing from sin is a far more urgent need, and yet how little used!

Like the leper we should say to Jesus, "If you will to do so, you can cure me." And our Lord's answer is, "Go off and present yourself to the priest." For in Confession the priest has the God-given power to say without ifs, ands or buts, "I absolve you from your sins in the name of the Father and of the Son and of the Holy Spirit."

Pope John Paul II gave us an Apostolic Exhortation on Reconciliation and Penance which helps us to appreciate even more the Sacrament of God's forgiving mercy. He states that the Church wants us to receive this sacrament more frequently, with trusting faith and no anxiety, aware that it is the ordinary way of obtaining forgiveness of sins committed after baptism.

He says that while the Sacrament of Penance requires a confession of sin and a kind of judgment, the confessional is a tribunal of mercy, not justice. A healing takes place there, a healing of a medicinal character helped by the confession of sin. As the priest St. Augustine said, "I wish to heal, not accuse." The priest and penitent are aware not just of sin committed, but of weakness and human frailty and God's great mercy at work.

When Jesus healed the leper, he took away both the defacement and the infection. In confession, God both forgives sin and heals the brokenness that leads to sin. The penitent's sincere and complete confession of sins is part of the healing process. It is also necessary so the priest can know the sinner's heart "in order to be able to judge and to absolve, to cure and to heal." Sometimes the priest sees that the penitent has not really come to repentance, and has to help him struggle for it.

Today's Psalm 32 is about a man who refused to admit and confess his sin. It caused his health of body and soul to waste away. Finally he brought himself to admit and confess his sin, and at last he found the peace and joy and exultation of being right with God. That is what a good confession can do.

But to gain this good from confession, the Pope says, the penitent must have a sound conscience, make a good examination of conscience, and have true contrition and conversion of heart from sin. As to a sound conscience, we must realize that sin is an act contrary to the moral law inscribed on our hearts, and admit that we have broken that law and put a large or small barrier between ourselves and God and also our neighbor.

The Pope says that even pagans were aware of these laws written in the human heart. Before Christ was born Sophocles wrote his play *Antigone,* which illustrates this. For political reasons, Creon the ruler of Thebes forbids anyone to bury the body of any man who was slain fighting against the city. Antigone, the sister of such a man, disobeys and buries her brother as reverence for the dead demands. To the ruler she says, "Nor did I think that your decrees had so much force that a mortal could override the unwritten and unchanging statutes of heaven. For their authority is not of today nor yesterday, but from all time." The Ten Commandments are such eternal laws.

In the Sacrament of Reconciliation the prodigal son or daughter turns from wrong ways and returns to the Father. He is also reconciled with the whole human family. He rediscovers his own true self and true way. He has the experience of being saved and freed by God. He is drawn close to the holiness of God against which he offended. This return to God is so personal that no one can do it for us, and so joyous that only the repentant sinner has ever experienced it. The Pope says that the priest himself must use the sacrament often or he will make a poor confessor and his parishioners will notice it.

Finally, as we turn to the Eucharistic Sacrifice where Jesus atones for our sins, recall the Church's teaching that frequent confession is an excellent preparation for the reception of the Lord's body and blood. After mortal sin, it is a required preparation. May God grant us the grace of frequent confession to share the holiness of his Son until our souls too shine with the radiance of God.

FIGHTING TEMPTATION

They tell the story of the polar explorer who was asked on his return what he missed most during his gruelling journey and he replied, "Temptation." And you may remember the humorous character in *My Fair Lady* who sings, "With a little bit of luck you'll give right in."

Once during the Civil War Abraham Lincoln told a funny story while he was waiting for his Cabinet to assemble. One member expressed outrage that the President should joke in the circumstances. Lincoln replied, "If I didn't joke, I'd die."

It's not wrong to joke about serious things; it's only wrong to think serious things are a joke. We may joke about temptation, but we know temptation is no joke. Anyone who forgets that is in trouble. At the dining club of one University the students took to alcoholic drink as a joke. Almost forty students suffered alcoholic poisoning and one nearly died. Real temptation is never a joke and if we don't recognize that we may pay with our lives, not to mention our eternity.

In Lent we have a special call to fight temptation in and with Christ. Through baptism we escaped the flood of sin and eternal death by entering into the safety of the new Ark, the Church which Christ built. But even in the Ark we have to fight temptation as Christ did.

We won't win that fight unless we have a lover's love of Christ and not merely a user's love. Users love Christ for what they can get out of him, the way we love cars. They want to make a servant of Christ. They want him to do everything for them, and leave them to do as they please.

That won't work. Christ defined a Christian as one who stands

by him and shares his trials and labors. "Unless you deny yourself
and take up your cross," he said, "you can't be my disciple."
Clearly, we need to love *Christ,* and not just what he can give us.
We need to long to walk with him, to serve with him and to do
spiritual battle with him as his friend and companion.

So this is clearly our calling and Lent calls us to reflect on it
and live it better. We have to know what temptation is to fight it.
What is temptation? How do we fight it and what are the rewards of
victory? Those are the questions I propose to answer.

First, what is temptation? Do you think those students who
came so near death from excessive drinking recognized their hour
of temptation? They thought it was all a joke.

What then is temptation? It's the enticement to live by any
way other than the way and the word of God and his Church.

You know most of us aren't going to do something wrong if
we know it's very bad. But if we really want to do it, we may
persuade ourselves that it's not so bad and finally that it's not bad at
all. The Jewish people have a saying, "If you do something wrong
the first time, it's terrible. If you do it the second time you say,
'What's wrong?' " To persuade ourselves that wrong is right is
what one priest calls blackjacking your conscience.

One temptation today is to dissent from the Church. Dissent is
the rejection of the Church's explanation of the word of God. Jesus
said, "Repent and believe the Good News." If we don't believe
the Good News, that is, the word of God, we can't recognize
temptation and so we can't repent. In the first Lenten Preface the
Church says of Christ that "By rejecting the devil's temptations he
taught us to reject the hidden corruption of evil." Evil often looks
as good as a shiny red apple until God's light reveals its rotten core.
There are many evils we can't know except by faith or by disastrous
and even irreversible experience, as Adam and Eve learned.

How then do we fight temptation? As Jesus did, by prayer and
penance and meditation on the word of God. Go in spirit into the
desert with Jesus during Lent. Spend time with him there during his

40 days and his temptations. Learn how the Commander in Chief wins the victory and imitate him. You'll soon grow and change and become more like him.

Recall that the first sin is what brought death into the world. Lent is a time to meditate on death. On Ash Wednesday we're told, "Remember that you are dust and to dust you will return. Repent and believe the Good News."

An Indian Jesuit, Father Anthony DeMello, recommended that we make a meditation on our own death and burial. In imagination we watch our body decay and turn to dust. Then we decide what we will do with our lives while we still have time. Father Anthony DeMello has since passed through the process he meditated on. So will we all. Now is the time to change what is wrong.

If you make that meditation, I recommend that you complete it with this one: See Christ coming and touching the dust and resurrecting you in the perfect body you've always desired, complete with the guarantee of immortality. Easter is a looking back on Christ's resurrection. One day we will look back on our own with all the joy that means. Let us now look forward to it and use it as strength for victory.

A sure-fire way to overcome temptation is to know how much God loves us. If we knew, we'd never betray him, any more than we will in heaven where we will know. Picture God saying to us what he says to his people through Isaiah: "As a young man marries a virgin, your Builder shall marry you; and as a bridegroom rejoices in his bride, so shall your God rejoice in you."

Thirdly, what is the reward of the conquest of temptation? It brings growth in holiness and innocence and eternal union with Jesus. Innocence is what puts sparkle and joy and spontaneity and gladness into life and limb, family and fellowship. Conquest of temptation restores some of that freedom and self-mastery which gave Adam and Eve mastery over creation until they sinned. It enables us to help others as Christ did. As St. Paul said, "Endurance brings tested virtue and tested virtue brings hope and hope will not leave us disappointed.'' It will lead us to life everlasting.

At our baptism we were asked, ''Do you renounce Satan and all his works and all his allurements?'' The answer was, ''Yes.'' We're called to say ''Yes'' with our lives this Lent. We're called to walk with Christ as Lord and friend, called to win the victory with him and walk with him back to the Father.

''B'' — Second Sunday of Lent   Gn 22:1-2, 9, 10-13, 15-18
                                                                    Rm 8:31-34
                                                                    Mk 9:2-10

THE MYSTERY OF THE GOD-MAN

A cone-shaped mountain named Tabor rises up just a few miles southeast of Nazareth, toward the Sea of Galilee. It is to the peak of Mount Tabor that pilgrims are led to commemorate the transfiguration of Jesus.

The events in the life of Jesus are mysteries we are called to meditate and share. To put it clearly: We enter the mystery of Jesus' transfiguration to be transfigured ourselves. Here and now, through Scripture and faith, we not only stand present to the Lord's transfiguration, but are summoned to share in it. St. Paul assures us that we can share in it, and tells us how. Gaze on Jesus, he says, and you will be transfigured into his image by the Holy Spirit.

Please note what this teaching means. It means that to learn of Jesus is to grow like him. Knowledge of Jesus is transforming. The meditation we are about to make on Jesus is not simply a matter of gaining information; it is a way of transformation.

Like the apostles on Tabor, then, we fix our eyes on Jesus. There Jesus stood on the mountain, a man with three other men. As the three watched, a glory burst from him, and the glorious witness of God the Father descended in the words, "This is my Son, my Beloved. Listen to him."

In Jesus' bodily presence plus the words of the Father, we have a summary of the mystery of Christ. He was a human being among human beings; he was also God among human beings — the Son of God who had become a human being.

Our task, then, is to get to know him better as true man and true God. We can gain knowledge of his humanness by paying attention to the Gospel people who give witness to their experience of his humanity.

The first of them is Mary. Mary carried him in her womb as every mother carries her child. She nursed him at the breast in his infancy. She nurtured him as he grew. Here St. Joseph, too, serves us, as he served Jesus. Together they witnessed him spring into manhood. They taught him, trained him, fed him when he was hungry, comforted him when he was hurt, and watched him when in weariness he fell into sleep. They saw him grow in wisdom and age and grace. Could they ever doubt that he was as human as you and I, though they knew too that he was much more?

The disciples too saw his work and his human needs, his sorrows and sufferings, his passion and death. In these are the clear signs of the human nature he shared with us all. From his disciples we learn how truly he is one of us.

Since Jesus was so human, we can learn of him by the very simple, very personal way of consulting our own experience. We all experienced what Jesus experienced — how it feels to grow up, to obey parents, to work and study and play and pray and make friends. All these things Jesus did.

Parents can go further. They have an especially privileged way of knowing Jesus. As they watch their children grow, they are having much the same experience Joseph and Mary had in raising the child Jesus. Through their own children they learn of Jesus.

All adults can go a step further. We share Jesus' experience of

going out into the world and learning to relate to society in the way
God the Father called both him and us to do — in loving service and
faithfulness to his law. By reflecting on this experience of ours, we
learn about the human Jesus.

Our further task is to know Jesus as God. The Apostles are our
help again. They saw his transfiguration and heard the Father
calling him his beloved Son. They witnessed him healing the sick,
walking on water, and calming the sea. They heard his declaration,
"Before Abraham came to be, I AM." And they saw him in that
final transfiguration, his Easter rising from the dead.

So far, we can summarize our faith in Jesus Christ in three
statements: As God's Son, he pre-existed everything created; he
became a true man; he rose from the dead.

But we can go yet further by drawing on the Church's 2,000
years of meditation on the mystery of Christ. Perhaps the clearest
summary is simply this — he is true God and true man; he is all God
is and all we are, except sinful. While he hung on the cross, dying
in his human nature, he was at the same time living eternally with
the Father in his divine nature. This is what the General Council of
Chalcedon was teaching in the year 451 when it wrote: "We
confess one and the same Christ, the Son, the Lord, the Only-
begotten, in two natures . . . this Holy Ecumenical Council has
defined that no one may advance any other belief."

There may always be those who will ask in disbelief how God
can be joined to man to become the single person of Christ. Long ago
St. Augustine answered by saying, ". . . as if they themselves could
explain something that happens every day, namely, how the soul is
joined to the body so as to form the single person of a human being."

This answer of Augustine not only answers the unbeliever,
but suggests to the believer how he can go deeper into the mystery
of Christ. God joined billions of cells, numerous parts and organs,
mind and will, passions and actions, body and soul to make the one
person each of us is. What then could stop him from joining
humanity to his divinity to become the God-Man?

In a brief moment we will confess that he did just that, by reciting the ancient Creed. United with Christians through the ages we will say, ''We believe in one Lord Jesus Christ, the only Son of God, eternally begotten of the Father, God from God . . . (who) by the power of the Holy Spirit . . . was born of the Virgin Mary, and became man.''

There is one final mystery of Christ to consider. Through baptism and the Eucharist he joins himself to his body the Church. St. Cyril of Alexandria saw in the Eucharist a clear argument for the divinity of Jesus. If Jesus weren't God, he said, the Eucharist would not be the body of God Incarnate. Holy Communion would not be life-giving, and we'd be mere cannibals. Here Cyril shows that the words and deeds of Jesus fuse into one and lead to only one conclusion: He is true God and true man, head of his body the Church, and Savior of the world. Today, as we recall Jesus transfigured and receive his risen body in the Eucharist, let us realize we too are being inwardly transfigured, in preparation for eternal life.

''B'' — Third Sunday of Lent

Ex 20:1-17
1 Cor 1:22-25
Jn 2:13-25

SANITY ABOUT SUFFERING

In the Holy Land there are many shrines honoring places and events in the life of Jesus, but some are of doubtful authenticity. Tabor, for instance, is pointed out as the mount where Jesus was transfigured, and yet the tradition is not so solid as to give us certitude. But the location of the Mount of Calvary is so well confirmed by archaeological studies that it admits no reasonable doubt. And how right it is that we should know the exact spot where

Jesus was lifted up on the cross to draw all to his pierced heart.

The suffering of Christ on Calvary is at the heart of our religion. We have been redeemed through the passion of Christ. The Father willed that Jesus sacrifice his body for us on the cross to take away our sins. The Letter to the Hebrews tells us it was prophesied of Jesus that on coming into the world he would say, "Sacrifice and offering you did not desire, but a body you have prepared for me . . . then I said, 'As it is written of me in the book, I have come to do your will, O God.' '' Jesus carried out that will of the Father by offering his own body for us through death on the cross.

It was this sacrifice of his body, the true Temple of God, that Jesus was foretelling in today's Gospel where he says, "Destroy this temple, and in three days I will raise it up."

Salvation through suffering was a scandal at the time. The Jewish people demanded saving wonders, and the Greeks demanded saving wisdom. Neither people recognized the wonder and the wisdom of a suffering Savior. They refused belief in a God who loves us beyond all our hopes and desires, who loved us enough to become man and die for our redemption.

One reason for resistance to the mystery of a suffering Savior then and now is that acceptance requires us to face up to our sinfulness. By sin we rebel against God and deserve punishment. Jesus bore the punishment for us and made atonement for our sins in a way we never could. To accept his redemption is to confess that we deserve what he suffered.

But that is not all that needs to be said. The mystery of redemptive suffering is deeper. Christ Jesus involves us too in the work of redemption. We must contribute to it as well as benefit from it. At the hour of our baptism Christ set us aside to participate in his redemptive suffering. St. Paul says, "Have this mind among yourselves which was in Christ Jesus . . . who emptied himself . . . and became obedient unto death, even death on a cross.'' And St. Cyprian makes the matter unmistakable when he writes, "The sacrifice of Our Lord is not complete as far as our sanctification is concerned unless our offerings and sacrifices correspond to his passion.''

We should understand this instinctively. "From the very creation of the world,'' Pope Pius XI wrote, ''mankind has recognized . . . the obligation of making reparation.'' He urged reparation to the Sacred Heart of Jesus. We have a duty of repentance, penance, mortification, atonement and reparation.

What does this mean in practice? It means both passive and active suffering.

Passive suffering consists in accepting the troubles and trials that come from living life faithfully. There is the suffering of resisting sin, the suffering of work, and the suffering of sickness. There is the suffering involved in family problems and in all we have to bear from one another. We can cry with Jesus in his agony, ''Father, take it away,'' but we must add with him, ''Yet, not what I will, but what you will.''

Active suffering means freely and generously adding penances of our own to share in the fasting and watching and prayer of Christ.

There is still another vision of the meaning of suffering that has a prominent role in today's world. It is the vision contained in the beatitudes. They are the code of Jesus' own life and the code of the Christian. We are to be poor in spirit and not greedy, to sorrow over the world's evils and not just our own, to be meek and not domineering, to be pure of heart and God's children and his peacemakers. We are called to turn the other cheek, to suffer violence with Christ without growing violent in return.

In the novel *Proteus,* by Morris West, the protagonist has a daughter who is violated and tortured, and he responds with violence and murder. He confesses that though he paid lip service to the beatitudes he never consented to living them. Isn't that a too common case among Christians?

Do we, in our daily life, accept the wisdom of a suffering

Savior? If not, we fail Christ. There is no Christianity without the beatitudes. They are the Father's plan, lived by the Son, and passed on to us. And make no mistake, they demand suffering. Jesus said, "Blest are you when they insult you and persecute you."

We see today a will to meet violence with violence, and threats of war with a nuclear armament that undermines the economy, disheartens the poor, and hangs a terror over the world. Some Christians have abandoned the beatitudes and gone over to guerrilla wars and terrorism.

We have not yet succeeded in clearly defining the right Christian solutions to the problem of war and violence, but we can at least point out the conflict between the war-hawk mentality and the beatitudes of Jesus. We claim the right to defend ourselves, but the truth is that in this nuclear age we may be entering circumstances where we cannot both claim that right and imitate Jesus. When he was faced with his unjust death sentence, he refused to use violence. That is the mark of the Christian martyr. He or she goes to an unjust death without resort to violence. We are called to be peacemakers, whatever the cost.

Let us end here at the altar. Our bread and wine will become Christ's body and blood once separated for us, but now risen and immortal. We're called to put our own bodies and wills on the paten with Christ, ready to go the way of the cross with him for the good of all mankind.

"B" — Fourth Sunday of Lent

2 Ch 36:14-17, 19-23
Ep 2:4-10
Jn 3:14-21

THE CRUCIFIX OUR HANDBOOK

A famous artist declared that there is nothing more subjective than objectivity. The reactions to Jesus hanging on the cross on the first Good Friday are illuminated by that remark. The standers-by thought themselves very objective when they stared at him in torture and saw nothing but a man abandoned by God. St. John looked and thought he saw all his hopes coming to grief. Mary saw the cruel hatred of men but perhaps she alone also saw the love of God made visible in her Son. Jesus in torture saw the fulfillment of all his labors for our redemption. He tells us this in his cry, "It is accomplished!"

All who saw him thought they were being objective, but only Jesus and Mary saw the deepest level of truth — the mystery of God's saving love.

Unbelievers see our crucifixes everywhere. They think they are being objective when they call us morbid for concentrating on the sufferings of Jesus. Suffering is something sane men avoid, is it not? Then why remind ourselves of it? Why dote on it? Why do Catholics parade the crucifix?

Those questions call for answers. Jesus gives us the means of answering them in today's Gospel when he says, "The Son of Man must be lifted up, that all who believe may have eternal life." When we look at the crucifix with the eyes of faith we see Jesus dying for our sins so as to rise for our salvation. We look at Christ our Life to be healed of the wound of death which we got when by sin we exposed ourselves to the bite of Satan.

What else do we see when we look at the crucifix? We see Jesus our Savior speaking in body language of his love for us. It is such clear language that any child understands. "He has loved me and delivered himself up for me."

We see the evil of our sins, which have brought the innocent Son of God to this torture. We learn that what our sins did to his body, they do to us body and soul. They bring death and only his death restores us to life.

We learn love. How can we look at Jesus and not return his love? How can we remember he did no wrong and not feel compassion? And how can we feel compassion and not renounce our sins, the cause of his suffering?

This kind of meditation on the crucifix is called the science of the saints. St. Francis of Assisi was a master of that science. He learned such compassion for Jesus crucified that on Mt. Alverno he received in his body the five wounds of Jesus. There is a great mystery in this. Let's examine it further.

Non-believers think our doting on suffering is morbid. They think we are in love with suffering. That is false. Neither Jesus, nor Francis, nor any Christian wants suffering for its own sake. Suffering is not an end but it is a means. Only Christians seem to understand this. Jesus suffered to pay the debt we fell into by sin. Just as a thief makes up for his theft by returning what he stole, Jesus made up for the dishonor our sins show God.

Jesus embraced suffering, not to increase it, but to put an end to it. Those who avoid it at any cost only multiply it. One small sign of Jesus' success in ending suffering can be seen in the history of crucifixion itself. In the year 337, Constantine the Great, the first Christian emperor, banned crucifixion to honor the crucified Christ. How that must have pleased Jesus!

Like Christ, we don't want suffering as an end, but as a means. We learn from the crucified Christ to do what God requires, even as Christ did. And we learn from his example that we cannot do God's will without suffering.

We also embrace suffering to embrace Christ suffering. We willingly do what he did, to complete in ourselves the work of redemption. In the hymn, *Stabat Mater,* we say to Mary by the cross:

> Since those cruel wounds that hang him on a tree
> Are dues of mine, O share them out with me.

The crucifix teaches us to stand ready to embrace suffering not only to end it in ourselves, but to end it in everybody. The life of St. Francis of Assisi illustrates this. When he meditated on Jesus crucified, he longed to end Jesus' suffering. At length he realized he could do it only by ending the suffering of all whom Jesus loved.

The crucifix taught him and teaches us the Christian duty of helping the sinful, the sick, and the poor.

The crucifix teaches us still deeper mysteries. What is the meaning of the wound in the heart of Jesus? The Book of Genesis and the Fathers of the Church tell us: Jesus is the new Adam. He falls asleep on the cross, his side is opened, and from the water of baptism that flows out, and the blood of the Eucharist, his bride the Church is born. And so we love the crucifix as the source of our eternal life.

The Church requires the presence of the crucifix wherever Mass is offered. It reminds us that the Mass is but the crucifixion present under the forms of bread and wine. The same body of Jesus is offered. True, it is glorified now, and wholly present in both bread and wine, but the bread and wine remind us that his body and blood were once separated for us.

The crucifix also reminds us of the resurrection. In early Christianity, the risen Christ was shown on the cross to teach that his passion led to the resurrection.

But it is the realistic crucifix that best reminds us of his love for us. On one great crucifix his body is gutted, like an animal hanging in a butcher shop. It tells us that Jesus' worst suffering was of the heart. We tore it out of him by our lack of love. His body will not be whole until we are joined to him in love.

In summary we can say the crucifix is our handbook of prayer. It makes prayer easy. Like the Bible it teaches us faith and love. So we hang it in our homes, carry it on the rosaries in our pockets, and gaze on it in prayer. And in Holy Communion we receive him who hung on it with love.

``B`` — Fifth Sunday of Lent   Jr 31:31-34
                                                            Heb 5:7-9
                                                            Jn 12:20-33

SIN'S FALSE ADVERTISING

American products come beautifully packaged. They attract the eye and promote sales. Who would complain about that except when the product is bad, and the packaging is a come-on to a swindle?

One of the oldest industries is the attractive packaging of temptation and sin. Even language is manipulated to conceal the real nature of the product. One person will brag about his cleverness at shoplifting — meaning that he steals and adds to the price honest people must pay. Another will speak of an indiscretion, when what he means is that he ignored his marriage vows, turned unfaithful to his spouse, and broke a commandment of God. A doctor speaks of terminating a pregnancy. What he means is that he killed and dismembered an innocent child in the womb.

This tells us a lot about human nature. We want to be good. We escape the call of goodness only by concealing the nature of the evil we do. To sin, we have to blackjack our consciences.

The three readings in today's Mass deal with the moment of trial, the hour of temptation, and the evil of sin. They call us to expose the real nature of sin and overcome it as Jesus did.

Sin is attractive — no doubt about it. We are never tempted except by what appears to be good but is not, or by what is good, but not for us. Abortion may appear good to a distraught woman. It appears to be a way out of heavy burdens and responsibilities. But the killing of an innocent child can never be good. It is a terrible crime.

Similarly, marital relations are good — for the married couple. Use of sex outside of marriage undermines family life, corrupts man-woman relationships, and flies in the face of God.

Property is good, but getting it by theft robs another of the reward of his labors. Sin is attractive only if we look at what we gain, and not at what we destroy. If we had and kept truth-in-advertisement laws about sin, sin would go out of style.

When we face the truth about sin, we know without teachers that we should never sin. In today's first reading, God foretells the New Covenant in which the Holy Spirit himself moves our hearts to the good. When we Christians sin, our sin is worse because we sin despite the light of Christ. We must avoid all sin, mortal and venial.

A mortal sin is one so serious that it ends our friendship with God. To die in that state is to be lost forever. Our Lord teaches us to endure anything rather than fall into mortal sin. "If your hand causes you to sin," he says, "cut it off; it is better for you to enter life maimed than with two hands to go to hell." St. Augustine explains that by your hand Jesus means your best friend. Jesus not only forbids sin; he warns us to avoid serious occasions of sin, even occasions as hard to avoid as our best friend.

Venial sins are those lesser sins, like lying and mean family arguments, which wound our relationship to God and one another. They pave the way to mortal sins.

The fight against sin can be disheartening, but we have strong remedies. The Christian remedy is to turn our eyes to Jesus and use the helps he provides.

The Jesus event in today's Gospel took place just before his passion. Some Gentiles want to meet him. Jesus finds this both joyful and sad: joyful, because it's the beginning of the conversion of the world; sad, because it means his hour of suffering is closing in. He is thrown into turmoil — that is, into temptation. He is tempted to run from his sufferings. But he sees that his whole life of faithfulness has led him to this hour when he must give everything, even his life. His coming passion will be at last the human race's full victory over sin and Satan. Satan will lose his hold on us, and we will return to God. He sees that when he is lifted on the cross he will win our salvation and our love. When he is lifted to resurrection he will win our eternal life. And so what he was tempted to run from he runs to.

If we look deeply into our own temptations we, too, will find there opportunities for victory. Temptation is a moment of choice. It is the noisy yet seductive voice enticing us to moral disaster. But from deep in our hearts comes the quiet call of the Father bidding us join Christ in defeating Satan. It is our hour to glorify God by our fidelity. What ennobles us above the animals is this power to freely honor God by our choices. Each time we say no to temptation we glorify God and make the world a better place.

From faithful Christians who have gone before us we learn how strongly we can line ourselves up for God and against sin. There are three degrees of this commitment to God. The first and lowest degree is to stand ready to die rather than commit mortal sin. The second degree is to stand ready to die rather than commit venial sin. The third and highest degree is to forego the comfortable way of life for sheer love of Christ. Those who take it freely share Christ's burden of poverty, suffering, and mockery. Religious set off on this road by their vows of poverty, chastity, and obedience. Married people do it by living the spirit of these vows.

Unless we have at least that first degree, that readiness to die in the body rather than in the soul, we are weak Christians and our salvation is in danger. But it would be unchristian to close on that note. Our salvation relies not on our strength and goodness but on God's. Our part is to be convinced that no sin is so small it doesn't matter, and none is so big that we can't turn to him in repentance and find forgiveness.

If we love God, we will sincerely try to avoid all sin. If we trust him, we will never lose hope no matter what our sins. God who is infinitely stronger than sin is on our side.

In this very hour we can take in our hands the unconquerable power for victory, the body and blood, soul and divinity of Jesus Christ. "Fear not," he said, "for I have overcome the world."

PROCLAIMING THE MYSTERY OF FAITH

Of all the times we feel the need of gathering together, the time of death is the most solemn and perhaps the most necessary. As a loved one's mortal life flickers and descends toward extinction, we huddle together to support one another in our bereavement and to join the candles of our individual faith into a pool of light that drives back the darkness.

At Mass, it is the Lord's death around which we gather, but it is also his resurrection. Today we begin a whole week of gathering in prayer and liturgy to proclaim that mystery of our faith. The week of Christ's passion began deceptively well, with his triumphal entry into Jerusalem. He didn't lack friends and followers then, but how many still stood by him five days later when he hung on the cross?

Are we willing to give special time this week to proclaiming the mystery of our faith? We have seen people neglecting their dying loved ones to go about business as usual. Perhaps we ourselves have been guilty of that shameful practice. If so, we can atone for our sin by not neglecting, this week, to stand by Christ in prayer and liturgy in order to share the mystery of his love and our redemption. If we want our Savior present to us at our death, we should not neglect his.

The liturgy of this week carries us deep into the mystery of our redemption. In the Gospel on Monday Jesus is anointed, and speaks of his burial. In Tuesday's Gospel he foretells his betrayal. On Wednesday he speaks of his way of suffering.

On Holy Thursday we celebrate the great and grave feast of the Last Supper. Once again he gives us his body, serves us through his ordained priests, and completes his gift of love by commanding us to love one another as he has loved us. This feast is so laden with love and memories of the Lord that it is a time of special graces and callings of the heart.

On Good Friday we do not have Mass. Mass is the offering of Calvary renewed, but on Good Friday we dare not offer Mass. It is as if on Good Friday Calvary bursts into every time and place so that we stand at the very foot of Christ's cross while he offers his sacrifice for our redemption. The account of his wounds and his death is read, and we kiss his cross and receive his body and blood in the Blessed Sacrament.

And then, in the evening liturgy of Holy Saturday, we make the final preparation for the glory of our Lord's resurrection.

We need to participate in both Passion Week and Easter if we want to join in our lives what no one should separate. When invited to proclaim the mystery of faith we say, "Christ has died, Christ has risen, Christ will come again." Thus we speak of Christ's death, resurrection, and return as one mystery. Without Easter, Christ's death would be in vain; without his death, Easter would be shorn of love; without his return at the end time, we would not share in his resurrection. These three are one, but unless we participate in them all they may not be one for us.

The mystery of our faith is the mystery of suffering love triumphant. Passion week is the invitation to share in this mystery to shore us up in our sufferings and our faith.

How many have ever understood the degradation and the dereliction Jesus endured for us? When Job suffered all his losses his wife cried, "Curse God and die!" Christ's sufferings were far worse than Job's. The ancient philosopher Seneca said crucified men cursed their birth, their mothers, and their executioners. Cicero said they uttered such blasphemies their tongues were cut out. And what did Jesus utter? "Father forgive them, for they know not what they do." No wonder the tough old centurion said in amazement, "Truly, this man was the Son of God!"

Even if we come to some knowledge of the physical sufferings of Jesus, who has ever descended the bottomless pit of his mental sufferings? He hangs mocked and tortured by the human race whom he came to redeem. His loved ones have deliberately chosen to be his executioners. As if this were not bad enough, the Father too has ceased to communicate with him and support him. "My God, my God," he cries, "why have you forsaken me?" This is the depth of the scandal, that we cannot tell from without and he cannot tell from within that God has not abandoned him. In St. Paul's terrible phrase, he was made sin for us.

Why did the Father ask him to endure so much? Perhaps another question will answer that: If after he endured so much we still waver in our loyalty, and perhaps even betray him, would there have been any hope of our response if he had not shown so much love? He suffered so much to release our love in return.

What did it cost the Father to allow his Son so to suffer? When King David's son, Absalom, rebelled against him and came out after him with an army, David's life was in danger. Yet he instructed his commander Joab not to harm the boy. But in fact when David's men conquered Absalom's, Joab killed the boy against instructions. When David heard, instead of rejoicing at the victory, he could only weep and say endlessly, "My son, my son Absalom. If only I had died instead of you." He wept on until Joab made him feel ashamed by telling him what his tears were doing to his faithful soldiers. After risking their lives for him, they were now so oppressed by his grief that they were slinking around as though they had betrayed him.

If the Father let us see his grief at the death of his Son, perhaps we would be too ashamed ever to return to him. In the beginning, after the fall of man, when God saw sin spreading, "he regretted that he had made man on the earth, and his heart was grieved." He sent the deluge to cleanse the earth. If we picture the deluge as the tears of the Father at the thought of his Son's coming death to wash away our sins, we would have only a hint of the truth. Did not the

Father, like David, have to conceal his sorrow from us, so that his tears would not undo the good done by the death of his Son?

Beginning today we are called to spend a week proclaiming the mystery of faith. Extra time spent in prayer and kindnesses, penance and liturgy is the order of the season.

"ABC" — Easter Sunday   Ac 10:34, 37-43
                                                    Col 3:1-3 or 1 Cor 5:6-8
                                                                  Jn 20:1-9

STRONG IN OUR JOY

Dear sisters and brothers in Christ, today we are called to joy. We are offered joy and given the privileged responsibility of cultivating joy. We owe it to the Lord to rejoice with him. He has died and risen for us. We owe it to ourselves. We owe it to one another as members of the faith. We owe it to the whole human race to cultivate joy in the risen Christ. Joy is important. It has many meanings and many powers.

The prophet Habakkuk gave a shining example of how to cultivate joy. He said that if the fig trees, vines and fields failed, and the herds and flocks disappeared, "yet will I rejoice in the Lord and exult in my saving God." God is the center of our lives and as long as we are right with God we have cause for joy.

The Lord is perfectly aware, the Church is aware, and I am aware that we all have troubles, sorrows and struggles with sin. There's no denying that. But our troubles are like a fly speck on the scales when we weigh them against what God is giving us this day. The mystery of the resurrection has come into our lives in Christ, and that calls for joy.

Centuries ago the prophet Nehemiah set the pattern for joy. To the people at a religious festival who wept over their troubles he urged a change of heart, saying, "Do not be saddened this day, for rejoicing in the Lord must be your strength." Yes, joy in the Lord is our strength. If you consult the definition of joy you can see why. Joy is that happy emotion that arises in our hearts when we're pleased with the way things are or when we have the expectation of everything our hearts desire. That last part is certainly the description of us Christians. Out of all our troubles the Lord is speeding us to resurrection and eternal life.

We'll look now at the joy which flooded the disciples on the first Easter, at the fact that we have like cause for joy, and finally at the fact that love of God is our greatest joy.

Joy flooded the disciples on the first Easter. Like some of us, perhaps, they were broken with sorrow when the first Easter dawned. They lived in a world that had hardly an inkling of the resurrection. It was only a dim glow even among the Jewish people. Then they had walked with the man who said, "I am the Resurrection and the Life," and their hearts were lifted on high. But they didn't understand his prophecies of his death and rising, for they stubbornly clung to their wrongheaded notion that the Messiah would never die. On that shocking afternoon when he yielded up his life on the cross their hope collapsed.

In the Gospel we meet Peter and John on Easter morn when they hear from the weeping Magdalene that now even their Lord's dead body is gone. They rush to the tomb and enter. John sees the winding sheets and the cloth which had wrapped his head. It is still wrapped like a helmet — as if, without disturbing it, his body had passed right out from its midst, needing it no longer. In a flash John recalled Jesus' teachings and understood and believed.

Later that day the risen Jesus stood in their midst. They saw the resurrection and it became the fact around which their lives took shape and Christianity spread to the world. Try to conceive and imagine the joy of the Blessed Mother when Jesus came to her. Their joy was one that even Adam and Eve in their happiest moments after creation had never experienced. That first Easter brought a joy the world had never known but would never lose again. Saint Augustine was only describing it when he said that a Christian should be all alleluia from head to toe.

Secondly, by faith and baptism we have substantially the same cause for joy. Knowledge of the resurrection has been passed on to us from the Apostles and the Holy Spirit gives witness to it in our hearts. God the Father has anointed us with salvation, washed away our sins in water, sanctified us in the Holy Spirit, made us a new creation, adopted us as his sons and daughters, and anointed us with the chrism of Christ. Made sharers in Christ's role of prophet, priest and king, we are joined to his life and called to his resurrection and the love of God in eternal life. Our salvation is secure, for Jesus said it is the Father's will that he should lose none of those sent to him, but raise them all on the last day. This is our faith, our expectation, and the cause of the joy that should flood our lives.

Finally, love of God is our greatest joy. We must open our hearts to love, for the prime cause of joy is love. Philosophers call joy a fruit, comparing it to what grows on trees. As apples grow on apple trees and oranges on orange trees, joy grows on the "tree" of love. To have joy we must cultivate true love.

The unfailing cause of joy is our love of God. By love of God we possess God here and now. God loved us before we were created, and that's why we were created. The moment we returned that love God came and made his home in us. We are one with him and he with us.

This best shines out in the Eucharist. At the Consecration the risen Christ will be present with us. In Holy Communion he will give himself to us as we give ourselves to him. That is our love and our joy.

Life is a struggle to hold to what we possess in joy. So St. Paul counsels us in the second reading to fix our hearts on our life in Christ, where we are hidden in God. If we let our hearts wander to trivial things, we will soon stray into endless sorrows. That is why we're lifting our minds and hearts to the things that really count, as did Habakkuk. Lent helped us do that, and now we want to reap the harvest of joy.

Today we recall our hearts to our risen Lord. He is leading us on the journey to resurrection and eternal life and love of God that will never fail. Let us address to him those fair words of Shakespeare:

> Thy sweet love remembered such wealth brings
> that then I scorn to change my state with kings.

As we turn now to the Holy Sacrifice where Christ will be with us, say to him, ''Easter with us, Lord Jesus. In Holy Communion, Easter heart to heart with each of us.''

''B'' — Second Sunday of Easter

Ac 4:32-35
1 Jn 5:1-6
Jn 20:19-31

THE JERUSALEM PARISH AND OURS

In the first reading, did you recognize yourselves — ourselves? For what we had before us was a parish, the very first parish. It's illuminating to learn how the word parish has been used among the People of God. The word comes from the Greek word, *paroikia,* which is a translation of the corresponding Hebrew word. Among the Chosen People it originally meant a sojourner, a temporary resident, a foreigner. Later, in Egypt, the Hebrews began to use the word of the whole people because they themselves had become exiles. When they returned from exile, the word continued to be used of them because they were in exile in the world, away from their eternal homeland.

That is the meaning the first Christians took over. They were in exile here on earth. That would be the people in Jerusalem whom we heard about in the Gospel. As the Church grew the word was reserved for what today we call a diocese; and finally it took on its present meaning: a geographical community of the faithful united, for the good of souls, under a pastor who represents the bishop in their midst.

Since we are a parish like the parish of Jerusalem, we can be illuminated by their activities and belief. They identified themselves as the baptized community of believers who had been reborn as children of God and were gathered around Jesus, the risen Messiah and Lord. They showed their fidelity by holding to the teaching of the Apostles and by loving one another and all others as well, for they recognized all were called to be God's children. In this faith they carried on their activities. They worshipped together as one, they lived in unity, and they were a ferment of missionary activity in the world. How could they possibly keep to themselves alone the salvation revealed to them?

You may have noticed one thing they did that we do not do in the parish today. In their fervor, they shared all their possessions in common. We have retained that sharing in the religious life, where it continues today.

Let us reflect on the activities of the Jerusalem parish, which remains a model for our own. They worshipped together, shared the one faith together, and carried on the works of Christ in the world. Because of their fervor, the faith spread like wildfire.

We have their inheritance, and we have their problems. We have the doubting Thomases which the Apostles had. The doubts are sometimes the same and sometimes different. We hear of doubts about the resurrection, doubts about eternal life, doubts about the authority of the Church to define faith and morals, doubts about the responsibility to carry on the work of Christ. What are we going to do about them?

Can you imagine the other Apostles saying to Thomas, "O.K., Thomas, your opinion is as good as ours"? Hardly! They reported what they had seen, they anguished, they argued, they prayed, they tried to convince Thomas. But notice what happened: It took the help of Jesus to convince him. We might pause for a moment and think: "These Apostles were no gullible fools. Thomas didn't demand too little proof; he demanded too much!" That should assure us that what has been handed on to us is solid and firm.

The need of Jesus to convince Thomas should teach us something. It is our worship together, around the risen Lord, that will bring us oneness of mind and heart. Notice that the one who was absent in the Sunday meeting with Jesus is the one who doubted. Doesn't that tell us that to be absent from Sunday worship is to open oneself to loss of the faith?

One thing we can learn from Thomas: He saw clearly that Jesus was the center of all they stood for. Without him there was no center worth bothering about.

Nor should we miss the charge of Jesus: "As the Father has sent me, so I send you." The sleepy, drowsy parish model of years ago when priests and religious seemed to be the only real doers never was valid and is now dead. The priest, head of the parish, is a helpless paraplegic if the body doesn't respond to his directions. What good are directions and warnings of dangers if the body neither does the deeds nor shuns the dangers?

The valid model of the parish is the model of collaboration. Every member serves Christ in his or her own role. A woman in one parish told her pastor how distressed she was by the bad radio talk shows in support of abortion. He told her to start her own program. She had no knowledge and no funds, but she tried — and soon had both a radio and a TV program. This is the way Vatican II approved when it wrote: "In the Church there are many apostolic undertakings which are established by the free choice of the laity and regulated by their prudent judgment. The mission of the Church can be better accomplished in certain circumstances by undertakings of this kind" (AA 24).

Think of the problems in our world: the drugs, the alcohol, the poverty, the moral and marriage problems. Do you think the priests can solve those problems? It's the laity who have the savvy, the contacts, the know-how, the means, and the call of Christ to work for change in the world.

In worship too we need the laity as musicians, choristers, lectors, Eucharistic ministers, altar boys, ushers, and others. Can priests and sisters operate and teach in all the schools, conduct CCD, visit all the sick, help all who need it, run all the organizations and start new ones, do all the parish planning, solve all the financial problems?

Know your dignity! You have been chosen by Christ not to be served, but to serve. "It is more blessed to give than to receive," for then you are more like Christ!

Finally, the parish is a family, and the high point of family life is the birth of new life. The high point then, is when our life, labors and witness give birth to a new member in the baptismal font of our parish. We should feel the joy of that event and pass out spiritual cigars. That is why the Church likes to see baptism take place at Sunday Mass. Then we see the fruit of the womb of the Church and of our labors, and are inspired to do even more. "A child is born to us."

In conclusion: Thomas doubted, then he cried, "My Lord and my God!" Then he rolled up his sleeves, went to work, and gave his life for the risen Christ. Thank you, Thomas, for showing us the way.

THE BIBLE IN CATHOLIC LIFE

"Thus it is written that the Messiah must suffer, and rise from the dead on the third day." God raised the body of his Son from the dead so that we will put all our hope in God. In today's Gospel, we hear Jesus using the Scriptures to confirm our faith. God is the perfect teacher. Through the prophets and the Scriptures he first foretold that he would raise Jesus from the dead, then he did it. Then he sent out eyewitnesses to give testimony that he had done it, and he appointed Evangelists to record it. So today our thoughts turn readily to the place of the Bible in our Catholic life. Here are three statements for a reflection on the Bible: First, it is the inspired word of God. Second, it can be badly misunderstood, so it needs the Church as authentic interpreter. Third, it does us the good God intends only if we use it.

First, then, the Bible is the inspired word of God. Vatican Council II explained that the books of the Bible "teach firmly, faithfully, and without error that truth which God wanted put into the sacred writings for our salvation." The Council added that, "having been written under the inspiration of the Holy Spirit, they have God as their Author." The Council went on to say that God employed human beings, with their talents and writing abilities, to write the Bible, but he inspired them to write exactly what he wanted them to say, as far as the revelation they contain is concerned.

An illuminating parallel can be found among human authors. When Fr. Walter Ciszek, S.J., returned to the U.S. from Siberia and that dread Moscow prison, Lubianka, he wrote a book called *With God in Russia*. Actually, he told his story to a competent writer, who wrote the book, but Fr. Ciszek's name is on the book as

author. In a similar way, the human authors wrote the Bible under
the inspiration of God, the Master Author.

The Bible supports our belief that God is its author. The
Second Letter of Peter says, "There is no prophecy of Scripture
that is a matter of personal interpretation, for . . . human beings
moved by the Holy Spirit spoke under the influence of God."
Clearly, both Scripture and tradition hold that the Bible is holy
because it is the revealed word of God. The Bible is *The Book* in our
lives.

Second, the Bible can be badly misunderstood; it needs the
Church as its authentic interpreter. Jesus himself indicated this. To
the Sadducees, who did not believe in the resurrection, he said,
"Are you not misled because you do not know the Scriptures or the
power of God?" The Sadducees had read the Scriptures well
enough to quote them, but not to understand them or accept the
whole of them.

Jesus entrusted the inspired word of God to his Church. The
Catholic Bible contains only the books the early Church selected as
inspired; it rejected others. Furthermore, the New Testament was
written by inspired members of the early Church. But these members did not write all that was known. The Apostles passed much on
only by word of mouth and the practices in the Church. What was
passed on that way is called *the tradition.* Without tradition, the
Bible cannot be adequately interpreted.

Only the Catholic Church has the whole and integral teaching
of Christ. It has the tradition, the authentic Bible, and the authority
and charism to interpret and develop its doctrine under the guidance of the Holy Spirit. All of the Church's dogmas and doctrines
are drawn and developed from the twin sources of Scripture and
tradition, which together are the "supreme rule of faith."

Word of mouth continues to interpret the Bible in the Church,
especially through preaching. The Church says that "the homily
is to be highly esteemed as part of the liturgy itself," for by
means of it, "the mysteries of the faith and the guiding prin-

ciples of the Christian life are expounded from the sacred text."

So here stands this ordained priest, saddled with the responsibility of properly, honestly, and knowledgeably interpreting the Scriptures according to Catholic tradition. This preaching role in the liturgy is itself a tradition that goes back to the early Church. You can find St. Justin Martyr recounting it in the Office of the Church for this day. Of course, we'd so much like to have the risen Jesus appear and do the interpreting for us, as in today's Gospel. He could do so, but it is not his good pleasure. However, he promised to join us when we gather in his name, so he's with us, and his Spirit is working in us, both to assist me, and to help you make up for my deficiencies.

Thirdly, the Bible does us the good God intends only if we use it. The Church certainly uses it. At every liturgy, it feeds us from the twin tables of the word of Scripture and the body of Christ. It is forbidden to have Mass without the scriptural readings. Sometimes tenderly, sometimes sternly, always lovingly, the Father speaks to us through his scriptural word. By it he gives us inspiration in every perplexity, help in every need, and consolation in every sorrow.

We read the Bible individually as well. The Bible should be the most honored book in our homes. We honor a book not by shelving it but by reading it. Let the Father speak to you even five minutes a day, and see your life change. But don't just let the Father speak to you. Read his word, then speak to him in turn. The Scripture is God's voice, and prayer is yours, and both should be heard.

Sometimes Catholics are embarrassed by Christians who make them feel ignorant by quoting chapter and verse of the Bible. Actually, you may know and understand the Bible better than they, for you've heard it read and explained all your life. If you add the hands-on experience of reading it alone at home regularly, you are the Bible Catholic we should all be, and you build a bridge to other Christians as well.

As part of the Church, the Scriptures help lead us to eternal life. Jesus once said to the Judeans, "You search the Scriptures, because you think you have eternal life through them; even they testify on my behalf. But you do not want to come to me to have life." We have come to Jesus. Do we come to him in the Scriptures as well? On this Sunday when we hear Jesus explaining the Scriptures, we could surely please him by telling him that from now on we're going to search for him and meet him more often in The Book.

"B" — Fourth Sunday of Easter   Ac 4:8-12
                                                  1 Jn 3:1-2
                                                  Jn 10:11-18

PERSONNEL WANTED

Every Sunday the "Personnel Wanted" section of the *New York Times* has a long list of job openings accompanied by fascinating job descriptions. No doubt these ads attract many applicants.

In today's Gospel Jesus gives a kind of "job description" of his priestly role. He gives his role a special title: He is the Good Shepherd. Please note that in describing his role as our leader he did not choose the word King or Master or Lord. He is all these, but he preferred the title, Good Shepherd.

The significance of that choice will be missed if we forget that a shepherd was a man without prestige. Shepherds had less social standing than today's farmer would have at a meeting of bankers, college professors, and doctors. Jesus knew that but still he said: "I am the Good Shepherd."

Let's consider why he chose that title by reflecting on his job description of his shepherd role. His job is to guard us and lead us.

He doesn't work for pay. He is faithful though he knows he will be killed in the line of duty. He serves all, even those who don't know him and those who don't want him. He has been appointed to this job by God his Father. He does his job with affection and genuine concern. Thus far the job description.

Now an announcement: The Lord's job is open to applicants. Men wanted. Who would want his job? The man who is speaking to you wanted it. He holds this post of Shepherd, and wonders why there are not a flood of applicants. He understands one reason for reluctance: the feeling of unworthiness. He himself dared to apply not because he felt worthy but because he felt called.

What is my role as priest-shepherd? It is to preach the Good News and the bad news as Jesus did. It is to tell all people of their call to eternal life and warn all of the danger of eternal damnation. It is to tell all Christians that they are already children of God. It is to remind them that as spiritual children they are subject to authority. It is to remember that the shepherd must exercise his authority to lead boldly, as Peter does in the first reading. It is to refuse to be cowed by those who denounce authority and equate it with the word "domineering." It is to know the difference between being authoritative and being domineering. The domineering person is arbitrary, overbearing and tyrannical. One who exercises true authority never domineers: he leads with respect but with firmness, in accord with the responsibility with which he has been charged.

The priest-shepherd is an ambassador of Christ (2 Cor 5:20). He obeys Christ by leading his people. In obedience to the revealed message he speaks with the Church's authority. He announces the good news that we are children of God now, and will grow into the mature likeness of God in eternal life. He preaches the "bad news" that we must renounce sin. He frees us for growth by condemning materialism, sexism, and infidelity to our sacred commitments. In all of this he imitates the Good Shepherd.

When young men hear the fullness of the Christian message fearlessly preached and see it selflessly lived in their own families, they too will respond to the call of the Good Shepherd, and we will have many vocations to the priesthood.

Once at Sunday Mass in a shore parish, a priest on vacation was attending Mass in layman's garb. The assistant pastor spotted him in his "disguise" and asked him to help with Communion.

Mindful of that event, I would like to ask a question. Are there any "disguised" priests in the pews? I mean future priests, as yet without collar, without ordination, without awareness, disguised even from themselves? If you feel the attraction to the priesthood, and have the aptitude for the studies, take the action of speaking to a priest. Don't be afraid. Don't demand more of yourself than Christ does. Some do, and it delays their response. Peter objected that he was too sinful, but Christ said to him and to all the Apostles: "It was not you who chose me, it was I who chose you . . . Come after me and I will make you fishers of men" (Jn 15:16; Mt 4:19).

All Christians are called to serve Christ perfectly. Priests are called to do it through committing their whole lives to serving as the Good Shepherd served. They are called to the bronze of chastity and the fire of charity.

The priesthood is a call to holiness, but not automatic holiness. It is a call to a manly struggle for holiness through serving others. Priests are kept humble by the holiness of those they serve. Benedict XV was a priest and a Pope, but on August 14, 1921 he canonized a saint who was neither priest nor Pope. He canonized Therese of Lisieux, a girl who had lived hidden in a Carmelite convent, and who died at 24. As Pope, he raised not himself but her to glory. Was not that act symbolic of the glory of the priesthood? "He must increase; I must decrease."

The priest is called to call all to holiness, for that is what the Good Shepherd did. He has a special responsibility to put before young men and women the call to the religious life.

Vatican II gave powerful witness to the special place of Brothers and Sisters in the Church. It confirmed what Catholics have always known, that the religious life of dedication to God in chastity, poverty, and obedience is a Gospel life. It is based on what Jesus taught and it imitates his very life. It is embraced to "derive more abundant fruit from the baptismal grace." It is a more perfect consecration to God. The life of religious Brothers and Sisters "reveals in a unique way that the kingdom of God and its overmastering necessities are superior to all earthly considerations" (*Dogmatic Constitution on the Church*, 43-44).

Brothers and Sisters have a privileged place in the work of the Good Shepherd. New pastoral ministries are open to them. New educational and training opportunities are available to them.

Christ is calling many young men and women in their hearts, and the Church is calling them through the preaching of the Gospel. I lend Christ my voice to say to them in his own words: "He who has ears to hear, let him hear!"

A privileged time to hear is when the Lord is with us in Holy Communion, for then he speaks to us heart to heart. If we all listen well today, we can hope to learn what share he wants us to have in his role as Good Shepherd.

"B" — Fifth Sunday of Easter

Ac 9:26-31
1 Jn 3:18-24
Jn 18:1-8

WANTED: A PEOPLE

Pope John XXIII once had a guest who asked him: "How many people work at the Vatican?" The Pope replied, "Oh, about half!" How, I wonder, would our local parish compare with the Vatican? God the Father himself is concerned about that question in today's Good News.

Jesus gives us good news today in the form of the parable of the vine and the branches. The parable describes the Church. The good news it contains is twofold. First, in the Church we are joined to the risen Christ so profoundly that we share his life-force. Second, the Father makes us more and more productive in and through the risen Christ. This mystery of union with Jesus in the Church invites us to ponder both our union with Jesus and our responsibility to serve his body the Church.

The union of Jesus with his members has two polarities. He is related to each of us individually, lovingly, personally, intimately. He is also related to us collectively. Depending on our own personalities and religious experiences, we tend to stress one of these polarities and to neglect the other. We stress our union with Jesus and neglect the Church, or we stress our Christian fellowship and neglect Christ. We have to correct such distortions. We are close friends of God and of one another in his Church.

Here is a statement which preserves both polarities of our relationship with Jesus: The Church must promote and not impede the individual member's relationship with God, and the individual is not to ignore the Church as his community. These two points are emphasized in today's three readings. In the Gospel Jesus makes it plain that the Church is not to down-play the individual's personal relationship with him. Jesus speaks expressly of the individual, of ''he who lives in me and I in him.'' He promises that ''If you live in me, and my words stay part of you, you may ask what you will — it will be done for you.''

Can we possibly grasp the joy of this good news? We are not merely being invited to fellowship with another human being. We are being invited to share the life of the risen Jesus, who is a new creation. Nor is he just a new creation. He is the Uncreated. Each of us in the Church has personal lines of communication with him, and a right to ask him personally for what we want.

No one may so stress the social aspects of the Church that he tries to talk us out of this Christian birthright. Pope Pius XII dwelt on this direct personal relationship with Jesus in his great encyclical, *The Mystical Body of Christ.* He wrote that "There are (people) who . . . spread abroad the idea that prayers offered to God in private should not be considered worth very much . . . Such an opinion is false; for the Divine Redeemer maintains closest union not only with His Church, which is His loved Spouse, but also with each and every faithful soul in it, and He longs to speak with them heart to heart, especially after Holy Communion'' (96).

This teaching strikes the right balance between our relationship to Christ through the Church, and our direct personal union with him. For who can give us Holy Communion except the Church and her ordained ministers? The Church is the mystery of encounter with Christ, just as Christ is the mystery of encounter with God.

Today we should ask ourselves: Do we have the longing to commune with Christ which he has to commune with us? One Protestant minister who has been in Communist prisons tells how you can distinguish a true Christian from a pretended one. He said when you offer a true Christian in Communist lands a Bible, his eyes widen with joy! I would add that Catholic eyes widen with joy when the Church gives us Holy Communion.

Now let us look at our collective relationship to Christ. The vine does not have one branch but many, as Christ has many members. The collectivity of his members is the Church, the people of God. God wants us to come to him not only as individuals, but as a people. Otherwise we would leave him out of too much of our lives, for by nature we are social creatures.

At this point it would be helpful to remember that the Church is such a mystery that no one model of the Church is adequate. Jesus himself presented many models. When he spoke of founding his Church, he described it as having an authority structure. He said to Peter: "I say to you, you are Peter, and upon this rock I will build my Church . . . Whatever you bind on earth shall be bound in heaven" (Mt 16:18-19). This model of the Church is reflected in the first reading. The Christians are afraid of the new convert, Saul, who had just been persecuting Christians. So Saul is taken to the Apostles, who make the decision to accept his conversion as genuine.

Vatican II stressed the model of the Church as the People of God. Only as a people can we support one another's faith, worship as Christ wills, and carry on his work effectively in the world.

This brings us to the second point of good news in the parable of the vine and branches: God the Father is at work in each of us to make us more productive. In what does this productivity consist? Jesus tells us, elsewhere, what constitutes its essence: "This is the work of God, that you believe in the One he sent" (Jn 6:29). In the second reading, John gives us a more expanded version of productivity: It consists in believing in Christ, keeping God's commandments, loving one another in deeds as well as words, and listening to our conscience.

St. Paul provides a model of the Church that helps us grasp what it means to be productive in Christ. He says we are the body of Christ. As each of our bodily members makes its contribution to our well being, so does each member of Christ. Paul's image helps us to examine our consciences on our productivity. Do I know my role in the body of Christ? What is it? Am I carrying it out? Am I serving the body of Christ in my family and my parish?

The bad news in today's Gospel is that we are in for suffering. God the good Gardener is trimming away our dead growth, so we won't waste the Christ-life. More terribly, he's pruning away the barren branches for burning. It's high time for each of us to ask: What have I done for Christ and his Church? What am I doing? What will I do? Christ wants to speak to us heart to heart in Holy Communion. Let us give him our answer.

WANTED: SPIRIT-FILLED APOSTLES

A bishop who came to a parish to administer the sacrament of confirmation first asked the children to define it. One child gave a letter-perfect answer, but the bishop put his hand to his ear and said "I didn't understand you." Another child burst out: "Bishop, you're not supposed to understand. It's a mystery!"

The sacrament of confirmation and the Holy Spirit who confirms us through this sacrament have been too much of a mystery in the life of many Christians. But in our time there is a hunger to know the Spirit and to feel his effects.

In today's first reading St. Peter himself is surprised by the action of the Holy Spirit. He is in the process of explaining the mystery of Jesus to unbaptized pagans. Suddenly, "the Holy Spirit descended on all who were listening to Peter's message." They began to speak in tongues and glorify God just as the Apostles themselves had done on Pentecost. The Spirit himself had seized the initiative and shown Peter the way: Gentiles were to be accepted as Christians without adopting the Jewish laws and customs. Obedient to the lead of the Spirit, Peter baptized those who had just received the Spirit.

You know of course that normally baptism precedes confirmation. It has from the beginning of the Church. For example, we are told in the Book of Acts that people in Samaria had been baptized by Philip the deacon. So the Apostles Peter and John went there, "imposed hands on them and they received the Holy Spirit."

This reception of the Holy Spirit in a sacrament distinct from baptism has been called the sacrament of confirmation since the

early centuries of the Church. In those days a Catholic was confirmed right after baptism. But in the western Church, confirmation came to be delayed after infant baptism came in. There is a
certain fitness to confirming the child only when he's old enough to
cooperate with the graces that call him to mature Christian living.

Confirmation is a resurrection-gift of Jesus to his Church. It is
a kind of continuation and extension of the Pentecost mystery to
everyone who is confirmed. In the new rite of the sacrament given
by Pope Paul VI, the confirmed person is anointed on the forehead
with the laying-on of hands and the words, "Receive the seal of the
Gift of the Holy Spirit."

On Pentecost the Apostles began at once to preach the Gospel
and spread the Church. Since confirmation is a kind of "sacrament
of Pentecost," it assigns all the confirmed to the work of spreading
the Gospel. It is the sacrament of the apostolate. The Council of
Florence taught that as the Spirit was given to the Apostles on
Pentecost, he is given to us in confirmation to strengthen us in
confessing Christ.

Vatican II taught that confirmation strengthens us in the Spirit
and obliges us to spread and defend the faith (*Dogmatic Constitution on the Church*, 11). It also taught that through baptism and
confirmation the laity "are assigned to the apostolate by the Lord
himself" (*Apostolate of the Laity*, 3).

It is important to understand how confirmation is related to the
"baptism in the Spirit" of which charismatics speak. Baptism in
the Spirit is a stirring up, a delayed awakening and experiencing, of
the grace of the Spirit conferred in confirmation. Baptism clothes
us in the "new man," Christ himself. Confirmation fills us with
the strength and power of his Spirit. "Baptism in the Spirit" is the
actual experience of living the life of Christ, the man of the Spirit.

To spread the Gospel by life and word takes strength and
courage. Confirmation gives us this strength and courage. That is
why the confirmed have been called "soldiers of Christ." This
description is valid if we understand it as soldiers of the Spirit. St.

Paul says, "The weapons of our warfare are not merely human. They possess God's power for the destruction of strongholds. We demolish . . . every proud pretension that raises itself against the knowledge of God."

The Spirit helps us battle for truth, which we propagate, not by killing for it, but when necessary by dying for it. The Fathers of the Church called confirmation the "sacrament of martyrdom."

In today's Gospel Jesus teaches many of these truths about confirmation in such a simple and fundamental way that we hardly recognize them. The key to recognition is to recall what John teaches us in the second reading: "God is love." God is given us through baptism into Christ and the Spirit of God is given us through confirmation. The Spirit is the mutual love of Father and Son. Thus the very "Love of Love" is what confirms us in Christ.

Therefore today's Gospel tells us in the most fundamental and irreducible ways what confirmation impels us to do. We are to live on in Christ's love, to love one another as he has loved us, to obey Christ as he obeyed the Father, and to lay down our lives for one another as he laid down his life for us. In all of these ways we are to "go forth and bear fruit."

We hear often of the importance of little things. In today's Gospel we're told of the importance of big things. Jesus never confined us to little things. Just the opposite! At the Last Supper he said: "Amen, amen I say to you, whoever believes in me will do the works that I do, and will do greater ones than these, because I am going to the Father, and whatever you ask in my name I will do . . ."

When Pope Pius XI canonized the martyr-saint, Andrew Bobola, he stressed this call of all of us to greatness. He described the tortures and torments that could not make Andrew deny his faith. He described his strenuous labors to spread the kingdom of God. He said these things remind us that the Church was born from Christ's pierced side and washed in his blood, and he added, "It has been truly said that 'Great achievement and great endurance are marks of the Christian.' ''

The Holy Spirit drew us together to offer this sacrifice of the crucified Christ today. Here, we take comfort and strength from Jesus and one another. Then we will go forth to serve in the likeness of Christ and Mary and all God's saints.

''B'' — The Ascension   Ac 1:1-11
                                                        Ep 1:17-23
                                                        Mk 16:15-20

THE EVERLASTING PEOPLE

To a little girl who asked if one might get to heaven in an airplane, the inventor Wilbur Wright responded, ''Not by going up, but if you have lived a very good life, you may do so by coming down!'' Today is the feast of Jesus' ascent to heaven, but it is really not about the mode of transportation. It is the mystery of the end of his visible presence on earth, and his entrance into the power and glory of heaven. It is our feast of joy at his happiness and our hope of one day sharing it. With silver trumpets Jewish priests used to send forth the sound of joy from the altar of sacrifice on great feasts. God calls us to this same spirit of joy today. The Prayer over the Gifts best expresses the theme: We beg to receive God's gifts as we celebrate his Son's Ascension, and strive to rise up with him to heaven's joys.

Our joy relies on the vibrancy of our faith-understanding of the Ascension. Do we grasp its meaning? We can if we reflect on the mystery of Christ, and of what awaits us in eternity.

The mystery of Christ is a great one. What does the Ascension mean for Christ? Today's Psalm says, ''God mounts his throne to shouts of joy.'' Does that mean Christ is simply returning after his time on earth, like a victor king returning? Or does it mean an original coronation of Christ?

We find help to answer such questions in the Christology of the Gospel of John. In the very first chapter John distinguishes between the eternal divinity of the Son of God, and the humanity which became his through his Incarnation. In his divinity the Son is unhistoried and eternal, forever seated on the throne of his royalty. In his conception and birth from a Virgin his humanity, like ours, had its vicissitudes and its history. Ages before Christ's birth God told his people: ''The land is mine, and you are but aliens who have become my tenants.'' Christ, like his ancestors before him and like us his members after him, was an alien and a wayfarer on this earth, in exile until he travelled home to the Father. The Ascension of Christ is the mystery in which his humanity passes forever beyond trials and beyond time to share in the lot of his own divinity and that of the Father. To answer our question, then: The crowning of his humanity at the right hand of the power of God is an original coronation, not a replay of something that existed before. We rejoice with the God-man because now, both as God and as man, he is in glory.

This brings us to the religious mystery of our own final sharing in the eternal lot of our Savior. In today's Gospel Christ commands his followers to trumpet to the whole world the good news. Spread the word that he has risen from the dead and ascended to eternity! Explain that even before he died he foretold his resurrection and ours. ''I am the Resurrection and the Life,'' he said. ''Whoever believes in me, though he should die, will come to life.'' At the Last Supper he promised to go ahead and prepare a place for us in the Father's dwellings, then return for us so we can be with him in his glory. This is his very purpose, to be our mediator, wash away our sins, and open all doors to our ascent to God, not because we first loved him, but because he first loved us.

In the first reading St. Luke refers to ''all that Jesus did and taught.'' Jesus repeatedly taught about the resurrection and life with God. He interpreted the story of Jonah's three days in the whale's belly as a figure of his own death and resurrection. He called us, his members, the ''children of the resurrection.'' He castigated the Sadducees for their failure to believe in resurrection and eternal life. He said it was because they understood neither the Scriptures nor the power of God. We have our Sadducees among us today, but if we have faith in Jesus we deplore their lack of faith and look with hope to the resurrection.

We look forward to more than resurrection. We hope to see the face of Jesus and the face of Mary with the eyes of our risen bodies; and the very face of God with the eyes of our souls. St. John tells us that ''we shall become like him, for we shall see him as he is.'' Pope Benedict XII defined the truth that souls in heaven ''see the divine essence intuitively and face to face so that. . . no creature acts as a medium of the vision, but the divine essence shows itself to them plainly, clearly, and openly.'' The God of loveliness will be the joy of our hearts.

These truths prompt us to confess in the Prayer after Communion that we touch the divine life now in the Eucharist. We beg the Father to stir our love to follow Christ into eternal life.

Unfortunately, some Christians use faith in the resurrection as a cop-out from their responsibilities. Some have used faith as an excuse for laziness. They lie about waiting for the resurrection. Of them Paul wrote: ''If anyone won't work, don't let him eat.'' Another example is the well-to-do person who exhorts the poor to put up with their lot for the sake of the resurrection, instead of sharing what he has to assure his own resurrection!

The Fathers of Vatican II exhort us to a realism regarding the resurrection. We'll be raised up in Christ, they wrote, but added: ''While we are warned that it profits a man nothing if he gain the whole world and lose himself, the expectation of a new earth must not weaken but rather stimulate our concern for this one . . . earthly progress must be carefully distinguished from the growth of

Christ's kingdom. Nevertheless, to the extent that the former can contribute to the better ordering of human society, it is of vital concern to the kingdom of God.''

The only right attitude is patterned after Jesus' own. He longed to go to the Father but first had good to do and a mission to execute. He expressed his love of God in obedience and his love of man in service. And he passed on those responsibilities to us: "Go into the whole world and proclaim the good news to all creation." And when the Apostles delayed a little too long at the site of the Ascension the angels gently nudged them with the words: "Why do you stand here looking up at the skies? This Jesus . . . will return." When Jesus returns he wants to find us not only waiting and hoping for him, but loving and working for one another. For his eternal life is already at work in us.

''B'' — Seventh Sunday of Easter

Ac 1:15-17, 20-26
1 Jn 4:11-16
Jn 17:11-19

WANTED: OTHER CHRISTS

Elijah the prophet and his follower Elisha were walking along together. Without warning, a fiery chariot swept between them and Elijah went up to heaven in a whirlwind. Elijah's mantle — his symbol of authority — fell to the ground. Elisha picked it up, put it on, and continued Elijah's prophetic work.

That event captures in a dramatic way the implications of today's liturgy. Christ has gone to the Father, and his role in the world is falling upon our shoulders.

We find Christ himself arranging for this orderly transfer of his mission in today's Gospel. The scene is the Last Supper, on the

night before he died. He is addressing a priestly prayer to the Father
for his followers. He says to the Father: "As you have sent me into
the world, so I have sent them into the world." Christ's sacred
mission is now ours, and he goes on to ask the Father to consecrate
us to the mission.

In the first reading we find the mission being taken most
seriously. The scene appears to be the same Supper Room. In this
event we are privileged to sit in on the council of the divinely
elected founding fathers of the Church. Peter is in charge. He
points out that to restore the number of Apostles to full strength the
traitor Judas must be replaced. If we switch for a moment to the
Gospel scene we find Jesus telling the Father that he has lost none
of his followers except the one whose defection had been
prophesied. In the first reading, Peter quotes the prophecies of
Judas' defection, especially that from Psalm 109: "May another
take his office." And so Peter petitions the Holy Spirit to reveal
who has been chosen in the place of Judas.

Peter doesn't know which man the Holy Spirit will choose,
but he knows the necessary qualifications. He must be a disciple
who was with Jesus and his followers from the days John was
baptizing to the day of Jesus' Ascension. His mission will be to
give witness to the resurrection. We ought to underscore that. Peter
identifies the apostolic role and the preaching of the Gospel with
the mission of witnessing to the resurrection.

Two men who qualify are singled out. Peter asks the Holy
Spirit to signal which of the two he has chosen, for the choice of
Apostle and priest is God's, not man's. The lot falls on Matthias.
Once again there are twelve Apostles, just as there were twelve
sons of Jacob and twelve tribes of Israel.

These twelve are the founding fathers of the Church by divine
appointment. The Acts of the Apostles recounts for us the building
up of the Church through their witness to the resurrection.

We are a hierarchical Church from the beginning, but we all
inherit and share Christ's mission of preaching the Gospel. How

are we to go about it? Today's three readings give us three norms: first, by witness to the resurrection; second, by consecration to the truth; third, by our manner of life in the Church. Let us look at each of these three norms.

We spread the Gospel by witnessing to the resurrection. We can't witness to the resurrection as people who saw it. We can only witness to our faith in the resurrection. We have become part of the unbroken chain of resurrection witnesses reaching back to the Apostles. We have inherited the sacramental mysteries by which we commune with the risen Jesus and feel his power in our lives.

How can we witness to the resurrection? Let me answer by asking two more questions: Are we free of materialism, greed and selfishness? Are we chaste and sober, pilgrims on the road to eternal life, rather than worldlings mired in the present? If we are, we are witnessing to the resurrection.

Second, we spread the Gospel by consecration to the truth. As we heard in the Gospel, Christ prayed to the Father and said: "Consecrate them by means of truth — your word is truth . . . I consecrate myself for their sakes now, that they may be consecrated in truth."

To be consecrated is to be set aside for God. To be consecrated by truth is to be made sacred by lives lived in accord with the Spirit of truth. Truth is sacred because it presents things as they really are. When things are seen as they really are, God their author is seen in them. If our whole lives are true, and if we constantly accept the whole truth the Church teaches instead of fabricating our own revelation, we will be credible witnesses of God and of the resurrection he promises.

An example of this constancy is given us by the priest, St. John Ogilvie. A convert from Calvinism, he preached in his native Scotland the primacy of the Pope in spiritual matters. He remained faithful through extreme suffering and martyrdom, and to this day over four centuries later he is attracting his beloved fellow countrymen into the Church.

Third, we spread the Gospel by our manner of life in the Church. What should that manner be? It should be characterized by love. For as John tells us in the second reading, the truth is that God is love. By faith in God's Son we are made one in God's Spirit of truth, and made one in his Spirit of love. Then we radiate the presence of God. Jesus said at the Last Supper: "This is how all will know that you are my disciples, if you have love for one another." If we love the Church, the body of Christ, if we love even the disagreeable and the dissenters, the world will know we are Christ's disciples, and recognize that we are radiating his Gospel.

We would love to be there with the Twelve and our Blessed Mother in the early days of the Church. We may think it would make everything easy. But read the Acts of the Apostles carefully, and see that there were disagreements and difficult characters in the Church from the beginning.

St. Paul said that we come to the kingdom of God through many trials and tribulations. It was true then; it is true now. The Holy Father sits in the Chair of Peter to settle our disagreements and lead us by the Holy Spirit to consecrate ourselves to the truth in word and life. Let us always remember that Christ is Truth, and we are gathered here to consecrate ourselves to him in the Father's name.

"ABC" — Pentecost   Ac 2:1-11
                                                    1 Cor 12:3-7, 12-13
                                                        Jn 20:19-23

THE DIFFERENCE LOVE MAKES

The ancient Greeks worshipped a god called Bacchus. They imagined him in the image of their own drunken orgies of wine and free love and other debaucheries. That false god, that projection of their own lusts, wounded and maimed a great civilization.

The Greek playwright Sophocles wrote:

> Great is love and what shall prevail against it . . . ?
> Wave of the sea is love, wind on the mountains:
> Neither deathless gods nor mortals escape it.
> The good it turns to evil, the wise to folly,
> All men to madness.

How different from this Sophoclean image of love is the Christian love found in the hearts of the faithful and crowned in the lives of the saints. The evil man it turns to good, the folly-ridden to wisdom, and all who receive it renounce their madness. How different from frenzied Bacchus is the God of love, the Holy Spirit, whose feast we celebrate today.

God is love, and Pentecost is the feast of the Holy Spirit of love. Christian life expresses love through the Holy Spirit's gifts. The sacrament of confirmation strengthened us in the service of love. Let us reflect on these truths of faith.

First, God is love, and Pentecost is the feast of the Holy Spirit, the person of love in the Trinity. Today is the feast of love in action. The Holy Spirit descends to bless the world with true love in all its healing joy. His feast completes the Easter cycle. He carries on the work of Jesus. He gives us in Christ's Church the gifts that send us out to reveal the God-Savior to all peoples and call all to one faith.

Through the breath of the Holy Spirit the atoning life of Jesus forgives sin and takes us into the Father's love complete. Pentecost is the very feast of the Father's love given us. When Jesus his Son ascended to him, the Father's love burst all barriers and roared down irresistibly upon the earth.

Our life in the Holy Spirit expresses this love through the Holy Spirit's gifts. The Holy Spirit gives each of us all that is needed to live the life of love. St. Paul describes what that life looks like. We become selfless, not self-serving. We grow patient and kind and shun rudeness. We look away from the failings of others, knowing only too well our own faults and sins. We attend only to the giving of love, hoping that when we fail others will be patient with us. We know that without love the most grandiose acts are worthless, including martyrdom itself. Only those who love are like God.

Love converts life in each family and in the family of the Church into an image of life in the Holy Trinity. We know only too well how often that fails to happen. An article on child abuse reflecting the opinion of those who work with families states, "Something seems to have gone awry in society as a whole, in the family structure, and in the way adults relate to their offspring."

What has gone wrong? If we receive the grace we ask in the Prayer over the Gifts today, we'll have a partial answer. We pray that the Holy Spirit will help us to understand the true meaning of this Sacrifice of the Mass. The very word *sacrifice* reminds us that to love faithfully and selflessly we have to sacrifice many of our own pleasures. This Holy Sacrifice is the mystery of Jesus dying for the redemption of all of us, the whole world, despite what we the world did to him. He endured the suffering and continued to love and serve. And though all looked hopeless, see how many he has won to love.

If we are reflective, we realize that every lover must endure something of our Lord's experience in order to remain faithful. Because we're imperfect and live with the imperfect we must bear with sin and selfishness to succeed in love. Love in and out of family life requires sacrifice. When the spirit of sacrifice fails, love fails.

Just as clearly, what has gone wrong is that many have departed from God's revealed norms for marital love. A British newspaper criticized Pope John Paul II for his "18th century sex morality." The Pope's morality is not 18th century, but first century. It is the teaching of Jesus. Jesus too was resented for his "old hat" morality. His went back beyond Moses, all the way back to the creation of man and woman: "Let no man separate what God has joined." Unless we return to what God has commanded from the beginning, families won't be healed. Rejection of God's law is sin, and sin is the contrary of love. The Holy Spirit turns us from sin, calling us back to truth and true love. To be fair to the English, I report that another paper declared that if there were such a title as First Citizen of the World, it would certainly go to Pope John Paul II.

Thirdly, the sacrament of confirmation strengthens us in the service of love. Fidelity to love can make daunting demands. When true love and passion are one, as on many a honeymoon, all is easy, but when love and passion conflict, we can only cry out with the drowning Peter, "Lord, save me!" If we really want help, he will stretch out his hand as he did to Peter, and we will be secure. "Ask and you shall receive," he promised. The Holy Spirit's descent in the roar of power and the light of the fire of love assures us that pure love is stronger than all else, and that he gives that power of love to us.

He gives it to us not just for our own personal interests, but for the service of the civilization of love, the kingdom of the Heart of the Redeemer. Each of us has his own mission in family and society and the Church. By the Spirit's gifts, especially through the sacrament of confirmation, we can carry out our tasks in boldness and convincing power.

On this her birthday, the Church sends us in prayer as her ambassadors to God, pleading for vocations to the priesthood and Sisterhood and Brotherhood and apostolate of the laity so she may not fail in her works of love.

The Holy Spirit touches us with fire today, but we need not be afraid. The only thing he sets on fire is our hearts. Let us prove that fire by the way we receive the Lord of the Spirit in the Eucharist today.

"ABC" — Trinity Sunday   Dt 4:32-34, 39-40
                                                           Rm 8:14-17
                                                           Mt 28:16-20

THE SIGN OF GOD

Today we celebrate the deepest and dearest of all mysteries, the mystery of God Almighty. We celebrate as a people who have been given a privileged look into the depths of God. God has disclosed his secret to us in the Christian revelation. He has told us he is a Trinity of Persons: Father, Son, and Holy Spirit. He stands revealed to us in the family life of Three who are one in love. We have come to know the Trinity of perfect lovers who are the source and the goal of all life and all community.

We know by faith that the Divine Three are unimaginably one, and we wonder how. When we ponder the mystery, we recall that even human love brings union. It makes of husband and wife "one flesh." It brings into being the oneness that is family, church, and nation. If human love unites, however imperfectly, much more does the perfect love of God unite the three Divine Persons. And all the more so because they are pure Spirits.

Christians long ago reached out to find some way to express in humble human terms this deepest of all truths, and came up with the sign of the Cross.

Each time we use this traditional sign, we signify to the world the deep mystery of God. And we give testimony that we are a people who have believed God, and believed in his mystery. The sign of the cross is therefore a twofold expression: It is a sign of the nature of God who has revealed himself, and a sign that we have responded to his call to salvation.

The sign of the cross also has symbolic meaning in its particulars. When we say, "In the name of the Father," and touch our forehead, the head of the body, we are honoring the first Person of the Blessed Trinity, who is the Father of the Only-begotten Son. We go on to touch our breasts as we say, "and of the Son." The human heart is the symbolic center of our affection. It is a praiseworthy symbol of the divine Son of God. It is as if we were saying to him, "You are filled with love beyond words for your Father and for all creation. For love of us you became a man with a human heart like ours."

If we can apply a lesson from embryologists, we know that three weeks after the Annunciation his heart was fully formed in his tiny body in Mary's womb, as were our hearts in our mothers' wombs. It began beating then, and through the years of his life it beat out the many rhythms of our human affections. It throbbed with his noble love for the Father; it thundered with anger at hypocrites who would suppress the truth of God; it beat wildly with the terrors of the onslaught of death; but mostly it pulsed with the tranquil rhythms of love and tender pity for all who would come to him for deliverance, and not come in vain. And on Calvary he left us a reminder of his sacrificial love in the sign of the cross which we are remembering now.

We continue the sign of the cross by touching our shoulders as we say, "and of the Holy Spirit." Our shoulders, the strength of our arms, are apt symbols of the Holy Spirit, who descends in the power of God's saving help, like wings spread over the world. He descended upon Jesus in the form of a dove at Jesus' baptism, and strengthened him for his mission unto death. With the roar of a mighty wind he descended on Pentecost in flaming tongues that inspired the Apostles to proclaim the word of salvation with the boldness of love. For the Holy Spirit is Divine Love, and love is the power that accomplishes every good.

Let us recall, too, the times we dip into holy water and make the sign of the cross. Thereby we sacramentally renew the moment we were baptized "in the name of the Father and of the Son and of the Holy Spirit," as Jesus commanded. At that moment we were taken up into the Son as children of the Father. We were made inheritors of what the Son of God possesses. We were given to God, and given God.

That fact takes us deeper. The sign of the cross is a call into the mystery of love. It tantalizes us with the joy of what we already know and stirs the longing to know more. It calls us to probe the mystery of the Father and all that comes from him; it moves us to share the love of the Son and all he gained for us; it summons us to lift our arms and carry on his work in the power of the Holy Spirit.

What is the sign of the cross? It is the sign and symbol of the beatific vision. It begins with faith and grows until the moment we will see the unity in Trinity in which we only believed, and will even enter into the union. We will be united with the life of the Holy Trinity. We will share in their family life forever.

Only, let us not think we have to wait until then to begin. Here today, by grace, we are joined to one another as members of God's family in Christ. Here today, in the Eucharist, we will be offered union with the divine Son, who is always present with the Father. If we live a devout life, we should experience in Holy Communion, at least at times, a taste of the joys awaiting us.

A young woman converted to Catholicism couldn't wait to receive her First Communion. When she did, she had no special consolations or experiences, but it was enough that Jesus had come into her life. Eventually she joined the Poor Clares and took the name "Sister Mary of the Holy Trinity." She found Confession hard, and once had to return to correct what she felt she had not properly explained the first time. Then she quickly went to receive Holy Communion, and of that Communion she said, "It was as though I had swallowed some of the sun!"

In faith, let us swallow the "sun" today, knowing that it will bring us to the light of the most Holy Trinity forever.

''B'' — Corpus Christi   Ex 24:3-8
Heb 9:11-15
Mk 14:12-16, 22-26

CELEBRATING OUR FOOD OF LIFE

We have so many concerns and troubles and attachments in life that we really have to make an effort on a great feast like Corpus Christi to cross over the bridge of faith into the eternal mysteries we are here to consider and to live. Because that bridge is one each of us constructs in part for himself, it can be pretty rickety; but let us cross over with trust in God, without whose help we cannot have faith. Then, for the love of Christ, we will enter deeply into this mystery, wresting our minds from all the concerns which are going to pass anyhow when we pass into eternal life.

If we have family concerns, remember that this feast of Corpus Christi, the body of Christ, is a family concern too. In the marriage covenant, husband and wife and children share family life together. By the covenant of the body and blood of Christ, we live together as the family of God.

The feast of the body and blood of Christ sets before us too many riches to appreciate fully. It reminds us of the Son of God's Incarnation and birth as man, and of his lovely human mother, Mary; it recalls the Last Supper, where he gave us this great gift of his body and blood in Holy Communion, the Sacrifice of the Mass he instituted there, his sacrifice on the cross the next day, the resurrection of his body from the dead, and his Ascension to the Father in heaven.

Here, let us concentrate on the body and blood of Christ as Holy Communion. In the other sacraments, Jesus gives us grace, but in this sacrament he gives us love, gives us himself, the Lord of grace. With that gift, everything is given, but it takes time to unveil and unfold. It is the sacrament of the future, for it is the source of our future development, our resurrection life, and our immortality.

To receive Holy Communion is to become united with Jesus, the God-man, in an indescribable way. As eating food unites us with what we eat, eating the bread of life unites us with Jesus, but in a more wonderful way. In today's Communion Antiphon, Jesus says, "Whoever eats my flesh and drinks my blood will live on in me and I in him."

St. Cyril of Alexandria reached out for ways of explaining the depths of this mystery. He said it's like yeast entering every part of the dough, and raising the whole loaf; and it's like two candles melted together into one piece of wax. We become united with Christ so profoundly that we share his life.

So we should see the greatness of this sacrament and receive it as often as possible. The ideal is that at every Mass the priest consecrates enough bread for each who will receive. The priest does not know which host is consecrated for you, but Jesus does. Has the Bread of Life which Jesus prepared for you ever been left unreceived by you?

How often should we receive? Jesus hints at the answer by giving himself under the form of bread and wine. Don't we need to eat and drink every day? Popes and saints have urged us to daily Communion.

When the shepherd boy, St. Paschal Baylon, heard the church bell ring for Mass, he had to stay and tend his sheep; so he knelt in the grass and joined himself to the Mass and asked Jesus to come spiritually into his heart. Can't we all do at least that every day? We can say, "Lord, I long to be there for that sacred Host where you become present for me alone, but my responsibilities prevent it. Come to me in spiritual communion."

We should prepare with great devotion for Holy Communion. We do all we can, and leave the rest to the Lord. In today's Gospel, Jesus tells his Apostles to prepare the place of the Last Supper for him by following the one who carries a water jar. We are that place, and the water jar is a symbol of our baptism. Jesus said they would find "an upstairs room, spacious, furnished, and all in order." That is the way the "upstairs room" of our souls should be when he comes.

Once, a group of priests went to a shore house to make a retreat. A doorknob came off in the hand, the dishwasher broke down, doors and windows stuck, and junk that had not been discarded lay about. One priest spent all his spare time making repairs and putting the place in order.

Jesus does the same when he comes to us in Holy Communion. Mary Magdalene thought the risen Jesus was the gardener. He *is* the gardener, and the repairman too, of the house which each of us is, the temple of God. Where the door of charity hangs off its hinges, he repairs it; the windows of faith clouded with dirt, he cleans; the house that is cold because the fire of love has almost died, he warms with the kindling wood of devotion.

If, the next time he comes, he finds things as bad as the last, it must be pretty disheartening. Let us be sure to help his work, and make ourselves homes worthy of him. We don't want him to have to roll up his sleeves and carry out the trash of pride, covetousness, lust, anger, gluttony, envy and sloth. We want him to find the banquet of love and the flowers of virtue that he found in Mary of Bethany's house, so that he can recline and speak to us of his love. And before he leaves, he will adorn our souls with more beauty than ever, and invite his Father to join him. So pleasing will we be, he will never leave us.

And now a special tip: Each time, before Holy Communion, ask our Blessed Mother to do a little house-cleaning. Then beg her to accompany him when he comes. With her presence making the whole place glow, how can Jesus help enjoying his visit, even if our souls are only humble little huts?

When Jesus comes, never fail to make "communion after Communion" — that is, to enter into exchanges with him. Who of us would invite a dear guest to our home, and the moment that guest arrives, say, "Nice to see you, but I have to rush out"? Can you imagine Martha or Mary doing that? Who of us would do that to a dear friend? When Jesus comes in Communion, let us make sure there *is* a communion.

The Church prays on the feast of the Visitation that we may recognize Jesus in the Eucharist as John the Baptist recognized him in Mary's womb. The Eucharistic Jesus is in the womb of the Church. Let's find him there with joy and gladness today.

"B" — Tenth Sunday of the Year

Gn 3:9-15
2 Cor 4:13-5:1
Mk 3:20-35

GETTING INTO SUNDAY

Like his stars shining day and night, God is present to us always; but just as we can't see the stars in daylight except from a deep well which filters out the sunlight, we don't always sense the presence of God. Only from the deep well of recollection which filters out the affairs of earth do we find him. That is why God has given us Sunday.

Every instructed Catholic knows of the serious obligation to attend Mass on Sunday. Taking that for granted, let us consider how to get into Sunday and get from it all God intends.

God has given us Sunday as the day to put aside all else so that his eternal light will flood our lives. But it's easy to spoil God's plan. It's not enough to go to Mass as required if we treat the rest of the day as a holiday unconnected with God. We'll find help to really getting into Sunday by looking to its origin.

Sunday's roots are in the Jewish Sabbath. If a Quiz Master asked the question, "Who celebrated the first Sabbath?", someone might answer, "Moses received the commandments, and the third is, 'Keep holy the Sabbath,' so perhaps it was Moses.'' But in fact, when God gave Moses that commandment, here is what he added: ''In six days the Lord made the heavens and the earth, the sea and all that is in them; but on the seventh day he rested. That is why the Lord has blessed the Sabbath day and made it holy.''

God himself first observed the Sabbath! His Sabbath law is a command to be like him. After creating, he rested and took joy in his work. The Sabbath calls to meditation on the wonders of creation and the divine presence that fills it. Relief from daily work, pressures and obligations makes that possible.

In another passage God says the Sabbath is the day to praise him for powerfully delivering his people from slavery in Egypt. The Sabbath, he says, is for slaves as well as for slave owners, for aliens as well as for Israelites, for beasts as well as for human beings. See here the kindness of God. He commanded a day of rest for the living, knowing our weakness and needs. If we don't rest we not only disobey his command but treat ourselves worse than we are supposed to treat a beast of burden.

The Sabbath is one of the finest gifts God and religion have given to this poor world. The great English jurist, Blackstone, said, ''The keeping one day in the seven holy, as a time of relaxation and refreshment as well as for public worship, is of admirable service to a state considered merely as a civil institution. It humanizes. . .''

Jesus rejected the Jewish laws which too much restricted Sabbath activities and harmed its joy. ''The Sabbath,'' he said, ''was made for man, not man for the Sabbath.'' He made it clear that necessary activities, and lending a hand to those who need it, chime right in with the Sabbath spirit.

Sunday takes up and surpasses the meaning of the Sabbath. Jesus passed over from the slavery of death to resurrection on Sunday, so Christians transferred their worship to that day when they assembled as his Church. They offered Mass to celebrate his conquest of death. They received the Eucharist to commune with him in his risen body, and found there a foretaste of his Second

Coming. They saw in Sunday the day God began the first creation, and the day Jesus began the new creation by his resurrection. And not forgetting practical matters of charity, they took up a collection for the Church and the poor.

The whole of God's special day is to be kept holy. That doesn't exclude healthful recreation. Many of us remember Sunday as a kind of father's day, when dad spent the whole day with mother and kids on outings or games, and in togetherness at home That is truly in the Sunday spirit, but there is more to it.

St. Thomas Aquinas taught that God forbids Sabbath work so that we will turn our lives from worldly to divine things. Sunday can be like a visit to our home in heaven for a day. The parish priest, St. John Vianney, said, "Through prayer we receive a foretaste of heaven and something of paradise comes down on us."

Sunday is a day to rest and read the Scriptures and ponder one's fate and one's God and fidelity to him. Adam blamed Eve for the fall, and Eve blamed the serpent. Both chose to believe someone else rather than God. Jesus came to defeat Satan and was attacked as his ally. The same deceits go on and on. We have to take time to think, to pray, to look for the truth in all things. We think about life and its meaning, about aging and dying. We stir faith in the resurrection, and find the joy of looking beyond what we see to the unseen delights God has promised.

Devout attendance at Mass helps us enter the unseen world of God. In the Post-Communion Prayer of one Mass we pray, "Lord, may the mysteries we receive prepare us for the eternal joys . . ." How do they prepare us? By giving us a foretaste of heaven that stirs our love and increases our faith and hope.

Church law makes Sunday Mass obligatory, but this law is more a reminder of an obligation than a cause of one. It's a filial duty of love and gratitude we owe the heavenly Father. It is a necessity. God requires that his children sit down and eat the divine food without which they would die a spiritual death.

The Church also says we must abstain from the "labors and

business concerns which impede the worship to be rendered to God, the joy which is proper to the Lord's day, and the proper relaxation of mind and body.'' Our Lord and his Church leave it to our prudent judgment to decide when there is work that must be done on Sunday. But if we're honest, we know that to really get into the Sabbath spirit as God did when he finished creating the world, we need to do what we can to make Sunday a real day of peace and rest and communion with God and family.

On Sunday we lay aside worldly concerns, wear special dress that says as much, slow to a leisurely pace, and live in a way which witnesses to the world that we weren't made for the world; the world was made for us, and we will outlast it eternally.

For our Sabbath rest, we can do no better than to take as our model the Holy Family. Would Jesus and Joseph the workers and Mary the mother and housewife approve our plans? Then let us proceed happily, with Sunday joy, in foretaste of the joy of our Father's eternal home.

''B'' — Eleventh Sunday of the Year

Ezk 17:22-24
2 Cor 5:6-10
Mk 4:26-34

WITH GOD'S EYES

''We walk by faith,'' St. Paul says in the second reading. What is it to walk through life by religious faith? Is it a blind leap into the dark, as some say? Is it an equally blind feeling for God? Is it a desperate act of pretending so we'll have something to cling to in a sea of uncertainties?

Before answering these questions, let's look at the three alternative ways of walking through life.

The first alternative is to walk by the light of natural religion. The natural religionist has gazed at the seas and the radiant skies and the wonder of living things, and concluded that you can't have creation without a Creator. And so he decides, "There is a God." He has seen for himself what St. Paul teaches, that "Since the creation of the world . . . God's eternal power and divinity have become visible, recognized through the things he has made." The natural religionist knows God without faith, by the power of reason. But because human reason is easily misled, the natural religionist's ideas of God are commonly mixed with error.

The second alternative to faith is the way of the agnostic. The agnostic doesn't say there is a God, and doesn't say there isn't. The world's evils, or his own, blind him to the evidence. He has no answers. He walks through life with questions.

The third alternative to faith is to walk the way of atheism. The atheist has a self-proclaimed dogma: "There is no God!" The Scripture says of him, "He is a fool."

So the alternatives to faith are to walk through life denying God's existence, or doubting it, or knowing pitifully little about God and his plans for us.

What is the solution then? There is none without the help of God, for there is no solution without faith, and faith is possible only with God's help. We can see this clearly if we consider that we can gain knowledge of God or anything else in only two ways: by learning for ourselves, or by receiving instruction from another. To gain knowledge in that second way is to gain it by faith in the word and testimony of another.

Let's take an example: A child is told by his mother not to put his hand in the fire or he'll get burned. If he believes her, he gains knowledge by natural faith. If he doesn't and gets burned, he gains knowledge by experience and reason.

Sound religious faith is saying "I believe you" to God communicating himself and his truths to us. His communication is called revelation. He reveals himself and what he knows and plans for us. If he kept silent and hidden, we'd be helpless, like children without instruction from their mother. We couldn't have faith if we had no word from God to believe. Oh, we could concoct something we imagined God said, like a child playing games of imagination. Only that wouldn't be faith. It would be self-delusion parading under the name of faith.

To make faith possible God communicates himself and his truths to us, and assists us to take hold of both. We can't do it unaided, any more than a teacup can hold an ocean. We need the help of his Holy Spirit shining in our minds. We call that help grace. The faith that results we call supernatural faith, because we needed God's help to have it. So faith is our response to God communicating with us. We say to God, ''I believe you,'' when he gives himself and his truth to each of us, the way he gave his Son to the whole world on the first Christmas.

I've repeatedly spoken of God revealing himself. How has he revealed himself? By his presence, by his powerful deeds and miracles as recorded in the Bible, by his word through the prophets, and finally by the birth and life of his Son. Jesus brings God to visibility, revealing himself to us in love.

Now let's go back to our first question: Is faith blind, or is it reasonable? When we seriously consider what God has revealed in history and in Christ, are believers blind, or unbelievers? Does anyone think Jesus ever asked his followers to act mindlessly? Why, he blamed them more for failing to think than for failing through weakness. He urged them to use their good sense to see what was before their eyes and accept it in faith. Faith can be the wisest and clearest-headed act of intelligence we ever make. St. Augustine says beautifully, ''Faith is nothing else than thinking with assent.'' Notice: Sound faith is first thinking, and *then* assenting.

If it is reasonable to believe human beings we trust, how much more reasonable it is to believe God, who supports his word with powerful miracles. St. John writes, ''Do we accept human testimony? The testimony of God is much greater . . . Whoever does not believe God has made God a liar."

To what do we Christians assent? To the evidence that God *is*, and has communicated with his Chosen People throughout their history; to the truth that God loves us, as shown by his powerful miracles and offer of salvation to all; to the fact that he has sent inspired witnesses capped by the coming of his Son; to the experiences of his care in our individual lives, especially through the Church Christ founded.

What then is faith? It's the act of believing God; of freely submitting our minds to his revelation; of knowing God by God. But by faith we don't just know God. We know what he wants us to know about life, and what he wants us to do until death, and how he awaits us with his gift of resurrection and eternal life.

We Catholics know the doctrinal and moral teaching of God with special clarity because we have the Church as our reliable teacher. We accept the Church's teaching authority not simply because the Church tells us to, but because God tells us to in his Scriptures and in the tradition handed on; and most fundamentally, because he tells us to in our own hearts. Awareness of this call to give the obedience of faith to the Church is part of the substance of the Catholic faith. The truths the Church teaches are so bound up with our faith that sometimes we call *them* the faith.

If we had a better way of walking through life than by faith, we'd take it. But who can propose a better way? The word of God says, "The just man shall live by faith." By faith we see, if only dimly, with God's eyes. What can be nobler than that? That's why, with our Mother Mary, "we walk by faith."

"B" — Twelfth Sunday of the Year   Jb 38:1, 8-11
2 Cor 5:14-17
Mk 4:35-51

LIGHT ON OUR PATH

We Americans never seem to lose interest in the stories of our frontier days. A central figure in those days was the woodsman who led the settlers on their expeditions. He was frequently a native Indian. Wherever they wanted to go, he could guide them. He knew the territory. He had been there.

Why do frontier stories carry such a charge of fascination for us? Perhaps because deep down we're all frontiersmen. Life is a journey into the unknown.

Our Christian joy is that in the journey of life we have the best of guides. Our guide, and he alone, knows the territory. He has made the passage to the shores of eternity, and returned to lead us there. And so we keep our eyes fixed on Jesus, "the pioneer and perfecter of our faith."

He has others in his service to assist us. Most of us took our first steps in faith with our parents as guides. It was their duty and privilege to shepherd us to Jesus and his Church. What a noble and weighty duty it was — to conduct us into the faith, the hidden wisdom of God, "which none of the princes of this world knew" until it was revealed by Christ.

At baptism we were given the gift of faith by God himself. We became "a new creation," as St. Paul says in the second reading. Baptized into Christ, we received a share in his divine nature and sonship and life and power to know God.

To be used, that power of faith had to await our growth in body and mind; and others had to teach us the faith, teach us the truths Christ revealed and gave to his Church. Christian education and formation were what molded us as Catholics.

The example of our parents was indispensable. Their lives, guided by Christ, guided us in turn. Then there were the priests of the Church who led us in faith and worship. And how fortunate if we also had religious Sisters to teach us!

We pause to focus on the responsibility of parents. Vatican Council II insists that parents have the "primary responsibility" to see that their children are educated in the faith. And be sure that a child's education begins by absorbing his parents' manners, moods and affections before ever they teach him his first prayer. If they are not faithful, practicing Catholics, there is no way they can fulfill their responsibility to Christ or to child.

And now we turn to the tragedy we see too often today: Some among us lose their Catholic faith, abandon Christ their guide, and wander into the swamps of disaster.

How do people lose their faith? We can touch on four causes: defective formation, erosion, hedonism, and confusion.

Defective formation results when parents fail to provide either good example or a good Christian education. Some children are not taught Christian doctrine either at home or at a Catholic school; others get the instruction in words, but not in the lives of their parents. If they see only money-seeking, pleasure-seeking, self-centered lives perhaps devoid even of Mass on Sundays, their faith is undermined. How often priests and Sisters grieve that their efforts are undone at home. And where priest or Sister sets the bad example, we can only think of the warning of Jesus: better if they had never been born!

If these children grow up and live immoral, drunken, or drug-filled lives, or drift into some strange cult in search of the ideal they never saw lived, those same parents wonder why. They neglect the hard fact that if they themselves escaped these excesses, it was because their own parents gave them a devout example in Christ which they failed to give their children.

Erosion of faith is also common today. Many reject demanding doctrine, forgetting they follow a crucified Christ. Desiring the way of the world, they reject the "obedience of faith"; but unable to live without the consolation of the Church, they concoct their own mix of doctrine. They receive the Church's sacraments and reject its moral teaching. They join the dissonant voices in the Church, and block out the voice of Pope and bishop. "Everybody's doing it," is their credo. But as St. Augustine said, "Wrong is wrong, even if everybody's doing it, and right is right, even if nobody's doing it."

Hedonism, the love of pleasure, is a disaster area for faith today. Immorality and violence and illicit sex pour into our homes on the waves of TV. We can dam those waves with a flip of the dial. Or we can terminate the cable TV contract, as one good father did. If we don't, we invite the evil they produce.

Confusion is a disease which injures the faith of many. The battle for faith invades the Church through the defective faith of its members, be they lay people, theologians, or clergy. Catholics who are illiterate in the faith fall easy prey to these false shepherds. So do any of us, no matter how gifted, unless we say with Paul, "I know whom I have believed." We have believed Christ and the teachers he sets over his Church in the line of the Apostles. They guide the development of doctrine and its application to complex modern moral questions. We have no mandate to concoct our own fragmented answers, or to turn to the simplistic answers of some fundamentalist Christian sect devoid of the full wisdom of Christ. Stick with the Church!

In the end, there's only one way to keep the faith. We need to believe and to know that, however hard the journey of life, we cannot throw faith away to lighten the burden. "Without faith," Scripture says, "it is impossible to please (God)."

Without faith we lose Jesus, our guide and companion. He walks with his Church to the end of days. He alone can teach us to walk in our new nature as children of God. He, the Lord of the storm in today's psalm, is our mariner and navigator. When storms of doubt arise, he stills both wind and wave if we cry out to him as did his disciples. He will lead us to our desired haven.

He who gave the seas their bounds is the one who invited us into the bark of Peter to travel to the farther shore. Even now he strengthens us through the feast of his risen body. Can we fail to desire the eternal life he shares with us, and to which he has pioneered the way?

If we see the irreplaceable value of faith and desire true life with all our hearts, we'll never lose the faith. No thing and no one will ever persuade us to abandon Christ, our beloved companion and guide, the pioneer and perfecter of our faith.

``B'' — Thirteenth Sunday of the Year

Ws 1:13-15; 2:23-24
2 Cor 8:7, 9, 13-15
Mk 5:21-43

BE COUNTED FOR LIFE

The radiance of Adam and Eve coming living from the hand of God is a theme worthy of endless meditation. The first reading summons us to that theme with a startling statement: ``God did not make death.'' God made man and woman deathless like himself.

The radiance of undying life is what we admire and long for — but perhaps not enough. Adam and Eve didn't admire it enough to keep it. They let Satan seduce them into an act that deprived them of both spiritual life and immortality.

God is life's giver. He loved us into life by acting creatively in cooperation with our own parents. He gave us a new life through baptism. He prepares us for a perfect life with him by resurrection in Christ.

Life is God's primal gift, the root of all his gifts. It is to be treasured in our own person and in every person. Every human life has equal dignity because each person is created in the image and likeness of God.

We have many concerns in life, but the first concern is to stay alive both spiritually and physically. Government's first responsibility is to help us in that task by warding off those who have no respect for life. It is a hard task today. Life is threatened at every stage. Abortion, infanticide, murder, suicide, starvation, and euthanasia crowd in on us. Nuclear war remains ever a danger.

Every one of these evils is contrary to reason and God's law. God gave us dominion over the lives of lesser creatures, but kept his ownership of human life. He wrote into human hearts the law of respect for human life from the beginning. He punished Cain severely for murdering his brother Abel.

In later ages when the law of the heart was dulled by sin God gave the Ten Commandments, of which the fifth is, ''You shall not kill.'' The accurate translation is, ''You shall not murder.'' It has always been so understood in Judaism and Christianity. And the Book of Exodus itself spells this out where it says, ''The innocent and the just you shall not put to death.''

Reverence for life was further enhanced by Jesus. He commanded love of enemies, and in the Sermon on the Mount he said, ''You have heard the commandment imposed on your forefathers, 'You shall not commit murder; every murderer shall be liable to judgment.' What I say to you is: everyone who grows angry with his brother shall be liable to judgment . . . and if he holds him in contempt he risks the fires of Gehenna.'' For, of course, anger and contempt are the triggers of murder.

Forbidden are all thoughts, false values, actions and failures to act that threaten life. Life is safeguarded only if we reverence every human life and promote a society that supports life. All life is God's and remains under his dominion. He gives it; he takes it back when he wills. Suicide and murder are great crimes and great sins.

We have many serious social problems to solve today. Let us look at four specific ones: abortion, euthanasia, poverty, and the threat of nuclear war. In searching for solutions, let us hold to the God-given directive that murder is not a solution, but a far worse problem.

Abortion is commonplace, and yet the more it spreads the greater its horror. Who is more innocent than an unborn child? Hear God's word: "The innocent . . . you shall not put to death." The Church has always abhorred abortion. The *Didache,* written less than fifty years after Christ's resurrection, forbade it. The Epistle of Barnabas, about sixty years later, declared: "Do not murder a child by abortion . . ." We recognize this teaching as that of our present Church. We cannot stand by idle while children are dying.

A *New York Times* poll reported that one out of every six Americans who agrees that abortion is murder also says it is sometimes the best course. Murder has now become a solution. No one who fails to resist can be called a Christian.

Now there is an effort to legalize euthanasia and suicide, so doctors may murder the old and the suffering who request it — and eventually, no doubt, those who do not. Yet who is more just than an old person who has done nothing wrong but to need care? What is more useful than a life being lived to the end in accord with the law of God? Are we not all pilgrims on our way to the Lord? Who is to say which part of our lives is most precious, or to declare any part of it worthless? Can we consider any suffering useless when we hold that the suffering of Christ — and ours in him — is the salvation of the world?

The need of the poor and the starving is another world problem. They are resented. Yet who has done less to deserve death than the starving multitudes whose only fault is to be born in poverty or forced into poverty? The Fathers of the Church said, "Feed the man dying of hunger, because if you have not fed him you have killed him."

Nuclear war stands in the wings. The popes and the bishops and our hearts show us the way to peace. It lies in the development of a world order wherein needy nations will not be driven to madness by unrelieved suffering. Until goods are divided more evenly through the workings of a more just society and a more Christlike people, the taking of life and the global threat to life will not be subdued.

These problems cry out to us to do more. The first thing to do — but not the last — is to examine our own hearts. Do we subscribe to any solutions that eliminate people instead of problems? In the final judgment of God we will be accounted worthy of life to the degree we counted others worthy of life by our thoughts, words and deeds.

In today's Gospel Jesus guides Jairus safely through the despair of the pro-death camp. He raises his young daughter from death. We can imitate him at least by standing against all despair and working to save lives threatened by death. Work for life is work for peace. It merits the resurrection life Jesus is so desirous of giving us all. Can we, who profess our faith in the triumph of life over death by receiving his risen body in the Eucharist today, fail to stand up and be counted for life?

"B" — Fourteenth Sunday of the Year

Ezk 2:2-5
2 Cor 12:7-10
Mk 6:1-6

THE WORD THAT SEARS OUR HEARTS

A priest congratulated an altar boy who served Mass well, and suggested he listen to see if God was calling him to be a priest. "My mother said I'm going to be a priest," the boy confided, "because I pray a lot and I'm always asking for money."

That is an aspect of priesthood, but there is the harder aspect treated in today's readings: the priest as prophet. In 1988, in the week preceding this Fourteenth Sunday, we saw on the world scene the recurrence of what is spoken of in today's readings. A Catholic bishop rejected Church teaching and went into schism.

If that were all it would be bad, but the crisis is broader. As one priest said, "The people are not listening." One mother told a priest of her unmarried daughter "shacking up" with a man on Saturday night and going to Holy Communion on Sunday morning. The distressed mother finally said to her, "Don't you think that is wrong?" The daughter retorted, "Why? I love him." That girl was not hearing God and his Church's word condemning premarital sex, and forbidding Holy Communion in a state of serious sin.

The crisis of faith in the Church is widely discussed. There are people who are not listening to the Word of God, priests and bishops who are not listening, theologians who are not listening. We must take the warnings in today's readings to heart. There are people not listening on the right, there are people not listening on the left, as has been made plain by Cardinal Ratzinger, Prefect of the Sacred Congregation for the Doctrine of the Faith.

The word of God is neither to right nor left. It is the prophetic word of salvation. Not to listen is to be lost. God's prophetic word is much different than many people realize. It is not always a prophecy about the future. It is his word about good and evil wherever it is rightly spoken on his behalf. The mother who corrected her daughter was speaking prophetically. In her role as mother she was repeating the word of God and the Church about what was wrong in the life of her daughter. And she got the rejection that Jesus experienced in his native town.

I will address three aspects of today's readings. First, the prophetic word is not of human origin. Second, the prophetic experience is described in the three readings. Third, we won't listen to God's word unless we do penance.

First then, the prophetic word is not of human origin. The Second Letter of Peter says, "There is no prophecy of Scripture that is a matter of personal interpretation, for no prophecy ever came through human will, but rather human beings moved by the Holy Spirit spoke under the influence of God.''

We are called to speak God's word by vocation or by office. By marriage a mother and a father have the office of guiding and correcting their children. As men and women of faith they have the guidance of the Church to carry out that office.

Priests are ordained to speak the prophetic word of God. A priest has his office by divine vocation. Its source is not any human gifts, but a divine call. Christ said to his Apostles, "You have not chosen me; I have chosen you." Before the Church ordains any man it examines whether he is being called by Christ.

It is God's will and the Church's that the priest preach God's word. This is what we must all remember. I am not here to preach my ideas, but God's word. Not every priest is faithful, and that complicates the problem for the people of God.

Secondly, the prophetic experience is the subject of the three readings. The reading from Ezekiel teaches us that God's word must be spoken whether people listen or not. God says to Ezekiel, "Whether they heed or resist they shall know that a prophet has been among them." Pope John Paul II is an example.

We priests love to please the people, but first of all we must please God or we are traitors to both God and the people. Pope John Paul II is perfectly mindful of that as I hope I am. And notice that priestly holiness or eloquence or brilliance does not assure a hearing. Christ himself was not listened to in his own town. Did you notice the little technique his townspeople used? They said in effect, "Who does he think he is, this carpenter? Is he any better than us?" They missed the whole point. That's brought out in the reading from Paul. The power is not in the preacher, it is in the word of God. Paul gave no credit to human qualities; he said, "When I am powerless, it is then that I am strong." If people listen to a priest because he is tall, dark, handsome and eloquent, they're listening to man's word, not God's. Listen to a priest because he speaks the word of faith, however poorly. It is our faith that brings us together and it is faith that is under trial in today's readings.

Thirdly, we won't listen to God's word unless we pray and do penance. We won't hear it though it rings in our ears. The Book of Wisdom makes that clear where it says, "Let us beset the just one because he is obnoxious to us; he sets himself against our doings . . . To us he is the censure of our thoughts. Merely to see him is a hardship for us." Isn't that the truth? We don't like to be criticized or told we are doing wrong. Even if we know it, the last thing we want is to be told about it.

The only solution lies in a change of heart. We have to pray and do penance for the grace to hear the word of God. St. Augustine says, "Men are hopeless creatures. The less they concentrate on their own sins, the more interested they are in the sins of others. They seek to criticize, not to correct. Unable to excuse themselves, they are ready to accuse others."

Our Lord said, "Unless you do penance you will all likewise perish." It is only moderation when we stop excessive use of food and drink; and only avoidance of sin to cease drunkenness and use of drugs. To fast as a penance means to eat less than we need as Jesus did during his forty days fast. Prayer, fasting and gifts to the poor change our hearts and make us sensitive to the word of God. We develop listening hearts, and then we are grateful that the word of God is preached to us in the Church of God.

This Sunday often falls close to the Fourth of July. We celebrate the Fourth only because those who have gone before us have guarded the work of the founding fathers and the words enshrined in the Constitution, so that the nation has not perished. We of the faith must guard its whole content and reverence the word of God or we will lose all that has been given and promised us in this life and the next.

Am 7:12-15
Ep 1:3-14
Mk 6:7-13

OUR CALLING AND OUR LISTENING

A priest one day received a shocking phone call from a young relative in a distant city. The girl was in a psychiatric ward, crying out for help. She was there because of drugs and drink. What went wrong? Whatever it was, it is going wrong with many across the country and the world. What went wrong? Let us learn from a comparison. Two friends had identical electronic typewriters. When one began malfunctioning, they put the good one beside the bad, and using it as a model discovered and repaired the cause of the malfunction.

What went wrong with that Catholic girl is that in the press of life she had lost Christ her model. If we don't pattern our lives after his we are asking for disaster, for he himself said, "I am the way."

Did that poor girl experience tragedy because she lacked someone close by her, whether parent or friend, to model Christ for her? Or did she have and ignore such a model?

I propose some serious thoughts about today's readings along three lines: First, our calling is to imitate Christ, and be patterns of Christ for others. Second, without lifelong listening to the Church we won't even hear our calling. Third, we each have our personal service to give God according to our way of life.

First, our calling is to imitate Christ, and be patterns of Christ for others. That we are called to imitate Christ is too clearly expressed in the Gospels to doubt. But we may evade its meaning by pretending we're capable of only a shoddy imitation of Christ. Paul shatters that pretense by insisting that "God chose us in (Christ) to be holy and blameless in his sight, to be full of love." Just think! God chose us before the stars were formed. Before the first star shone he was thinking of and choosing us to walk in his Son's likeness and share his life and sonship.

Do we set our sights on that God-given goal, or merely try to keep out of sin? God never told us merely to keep out of sin. He told us to grow full of unblemished love. He wants nothing less for us. Have we ever accepted his call?

Perhaps even harder, God wants us to be patterns of Christ for others. Paul had the nerve to say, "Be imitators of me as I am of Christ." If we said it it might ring false, or at least sound like bragging, but that's what we should be, isn't it? If a priest doesn't practice what he preaches, who listens? If parents get heavy into drinking, drugs, gambling and all that has no place in the life of a Christian, what chance do their children have? If a parent says, "Don't do what I do, do what I say," will children listen from the heart? It's clear, then, that our call to be patterns of Christ is non-negotiable.

Secondly, without lifelong listening to the Church we won't even hear our calling. Our calling is divine. It's revealed by God. We can learn it only from his prophets and his Church. In the first reading Amaziah the dissident priest thought he could do without the word of Amos. In fact, he insulted him by treating him as though he were prophesying to make a living. Amos makes it clear he was making a good living as a shepherd and forester until God called him to leave his livelihood to prophesy.

Once one priest told another of a seminarian who was working two months each summer to pay for his seminary training. The first priest explained that the seminarian was an expert in his field and said with a laugh, "He's making more in two months than we make in a year." Like Amos, that seminarian can set anyone straight who tells him he is preaching the word of God for money. So could other priests.

Amos was in effect saying to Amaziah, "In rejecting me, you reject God who sent me." Our Lord confirms that by his word to his disciples: ''He who hears you hears me. He who rejects you rejects me.''

Yet God's word in Scripture and Church is being rejected by many Catholics. In one poll more than half doubted the existence of hell and the devil, and doubted as well that Jesus had handed leadership of his Church to Peter and his successors. Will people who don't hear God's word in the Church ever hear their own call or be able to follow it? They're like a foreign ambassador who won't listen to a messenger sent by the president.

Thirdly, we each have our personal service to give God according to our way of life. Who can doubt that one of the most essential services to give God today is to be a good spouse and parent? On these depend the good of children and of all society. The young above all others need us as patterns of Christ. They need patterns in sobriety of life, modesty of dress, and concern to do good and to serve rather than to earn big money.

It's strange how many people act as if their relationship with God is just a Sunday calling divorced from the rest of their lives. To divorce religion from life is the formula for disaster. Christ is our life. Who ever heard of anyone doing anything apart from his life? Our success or failure with God is the only true measure of the worth of our life. We cannot fail God and the Church without failing ourselves, our children and our society.

There is one vocation we all have, to be a good son or daughter. Who can measure its importance? If we fail we betray Christ our brother, and break the hearts of our parents and our Father in heaven. Even if our parents fail to be the pattern they owe us, our heavenly Father will not fail us. His grace can make up for everything, as the lives of some saints attest.

Where we don't have good Catholic family life, how will we ever have enough priests, deacons, Sisters and Brothers? The Vatican has prepared a service for priestless Sundays, and there are already many priestless Sundays in parishes around the world. If you love the Mass and the Eucharist, if you feel the need to have your sins forgiven in Confession, and your body anointed in sickness, and your priest to witness to your marriage, know that vocations begin in good families, and live accordingly.

Out of the family come as well all the other workers in the Church. So today when we receive the Lord of the Eucharist, let's all pray him to bless family life, make it holy and happy, and make it the source of many laborers to reap his great harvest of souls.

"B" — Sixteenth Sunday of the Year

Jr 23:1-6
Ep 2:13-18
Mk 6:30-34

JOY IN THE GOOD SHEPHERD

As a mother on an ocean beach was trying to comb out the tangled hair of her little boy, he clung to her and moaned, "It hurts." And she said, "The tighter you hug me the better it will feel." That's the advice God is giving us today: cling to him, hug him close, stay by him. In that is our joy.

All the readings today draw us close to God. They invite us to reflect that God himself has become our shepherd; that if we knew what God has given us we'd die of longing to be with him; but that it's hard to make his words register with us.

First, then, God himself has become our shepherd. He promised he would in the first reading from ages ago. Angry with the unfaithful shepherds he appointed, he will punish them, and then himself be shepherd. "I will raise up a righteous shoot to David," he promises. The Jewish people recognized here the promise of a messiah who would be their shepherd. He has come, God has come in Christ. Tenderly he shepherds us through life to true life in our Father's home. In the Gospel Jesus, seeing the people like sheep without a shepherd, becomes their Good Shepherd. He teaches them, and he is teaching us still.

If we knew what God has given us we'd die of longing to be with him. Our poor mortal life couldn't sustain the longing, joy and desire to be with so loving a God. God wants us to get hold of that truth and experience the joy of his love. Through Jeremiah the prophet he says, "I have loved you with an everlasting love."

Now I know it's not always easy to be joyous. There are many sorrows in life. Jesus himself has been called the Man of Sorrows. Yet sorrow is not from Christianity, but from its lack. It's from seeing evil and infidelity and suffering around us and especially within us. So grief and sorrow come from human conduct, not from God. They come especially from not believing in the gifts of God, including unlimited forgiveness.

If we are sincerely trying to be faithful, Jesus wants us to have joy. St. Augustine said over 1500 years ago that a Christian should be all alleluia from head to toe. It's of course easier said than done. But at any rate please take note that the Lord himself made it clear that we are meant to be a people sharing his joy. At the Last Supper he said, "I have told you this that my joy may be in you and your joy may be complete."

Just what did he tell us that should be our fountain of joy? He said, "I am the resurrection and the life." And he said, "I am the vine and you the branches." In other words, he joins us to himself life-to-life, to share his divine sonship and his resurrection life. Since he was returning to the Father, he said, "I will come back again and take you to myself, that where I am you also may be." But perhaps most stunningly of all, he said, "As the Father loves me, so I also love you." Who can grasp that? Who has the faith and courage to believe it? I'll leave it to your meditation. It's like an ant trying to climb a mountain, an ant who is too small to tell a molehill from a mountain.

But I want to mention in particular three gifts that promote joy here and now. He gave us his Body and Blood which is now his risen Body and Blood. He also gave us his mystical body, that is, he gave us one another. He did that when he said, "Love one another as I have loved you." If we Christians obeyed that commandment and loved one another as Jesus has loved us, think of the joy it would bring us, and think of the joy we would bring others. And Jesus gave us the gift of the priesthood so that the Eucharist would be available to us.

Has it occurred to you that these last three gifts are all present here today? We his mystical body are present to one another. His priest is present to offer the sacrifice, and Jesus will be present on the altar. If we knew what God has given us in love, we would be full of joy, and of longing to be with him.

Of course, it's hard to make his words register with us. Someone here might say to me, "I don't disbelieve, but I just can't get hold of it. How can I get a grasp on it and really feel it so I may have this joy?" Perhaps the best answer I can give is one word, *Pray!* I don't mean just saying prayers; I mean prayer of thought and reflection on the word of God.

Today's psalm, *The Lord is my Shepherd,* teaches the prayer I mean. The prophet begins by thinking, "The Lord is my Shepherd. I won't lack anything. What I really need he is going to take care of." He goes on thinking along those lines, and adds, "Even though I walk in the dark valley I fear no evil; for you are at my side." Did you notice the striking change in that last phrase? He was thinking *about* God when suddenly he realized the truth of what he's saying: *God is with me!* So at once he turns from thinking about God to talking to God: "*You* are at my side!"

That's a perfect example of deep prayer. We begin prayer by gathering our thoughts together and gathering our wits and overcoming distraction, and thinking of what God has told us. All of a sudden we remember that you, Jesus, promised, "If anyone loves me he will keep my word and the Father will love him and we will come to him and make our home with him." So Jesus, why should I think about you and what you said when I can be aware of your presence and *talk* to you about what you said, and beg you to make it all register with me?

If only we could grasp what a tremendous gift prayer is! Let me try to help by a story. A man had a friend who was one of those name-droppers, always trying to impress him by casually referring to important people he knew. One day he said, "I won't see you next week. I'm meeting the President of the United States on Thursday at 3:35 p.m." His friend replied, "I'll be busy myself. I have appointments with Almighty God anytime I want them, day or night, and I frequently take advantage of it."

Did you ever think of what an unimaginable gift we have? Why should God listen to you or me any time of the day or night? Why? Because he loves us as much as he has said. If we pray well and often and live what we learn, we will come to a knowledge of his love and be inflamed with love returned. Prayer takes us to the ocean of God's love from which a river of joy pours into us.

Today our tender and loving Shepherd is calling us. In prayer we hear his divine voice, and sense what he wants of us. Love for his Sacred Heart wells up in our hearts, and it becomes a joy to do what he wants. Then we have not only a Good Shepherd but good sheep. Let us pray for that gift today.

"B" — Seventeenth Sunday of the Year

2 K 4:42-44
Ep 4:1-6
Jn 6:1-15

GOD: THE PROBLEM OR THE SOLUTION?

Summer is beach weather. Water and sun are a pleasure for many, but at times a danger. One day three young girls frolicking in rough ocean water were swept out beyond their depth. A woman shouted. Burly lifeguards rushed out. The girls were saved from certain death.

Do we thank human beings for saving them, or thank God, or thank both? Both Elisha and Jesus fed the hungry, but only by the power of God. Did the lifeguards do it by any power, inspiration or bravery except from God? Today's psalm says, "The *hand* of the Lord feeds us; he answers all our needs." Do we believe it? And realize the hand he uses is most often our own? In the Opening Prayer we say to God, "Guide us to everlasting life by helping us to use wisely the blessings you have given the world."

Elisha's servant said of the little food they had, "How can I set this before a hundred men?" How often a larger question is asked today: How feed the world? In answer, recall the word of the angel to Mary, "Nothing will be impossible with God." But also realize that God in his providence has given us intelligence and responsibility to use wisely all his other gifts.

Let us reflect today on the problems of being a world citizen, the inhuman vs. human solutions to our problems, and the need to walk with God, do our best, and trust him to provide.

First, the problems of being a world citizen. In ancient times, families often fended for themselves; then tribes gathered, then towns, then cities and states and nations; and now we're all aboard spaceship earth, our global village, with the news of the world pouring in daily. There is one body, one spirit, one hope, one Lord, one faith, one baptism, and one God and Father who works through us all (Second Reading).

But how many believe this, even of believers? Atheists think God is the problem, not the solution. Where do you stand? The atheist argues that the moral law which believers hold is the obstacle to solving our problems. True believers insist that breaking God's law is what causes the problems, and to break more laws to provide a solution will cause an explosion of problems.

So we're in conflict over inhuman vs. human solutions to our problems. Many warn of over-population and clamor for artificial birth control, abortion, mercy killing and policies even more un-mentionable. Despite forced abortions in China, the *New York Times* deplored U.S. refusal to fund China's family planning. Yet the United Nations admits that the world could feed more than double its present population, and a *Wall Street Journal* article said it would take a famine to sell the food stores on hand. The real problem is mismanagement, greed, and war.

The Church teaches that artificial birth control, abortion and sterilization are not only forbidden by God; they are contrary to providence, justice and humanity. In 1968 Pope Paul VI issued *Humanae Vitae* on "The Regulation of Births." He recognized the Third World population problems and also the need of authentic family planning for all married people. But he deplored the use of contraception and abortion as solutions. Prophetically, he warned that the consequences would be marital infidelity, decline of moral standards, especially among the young, lack of respect for women and women's health, and forced use of contraceptives by governments.

The decades since show that he understated the case. The divorce rate has risen to 50%; tens of millions of babies have been killed in the womb; premarital sex and adultery and the porn industry which promote them are everywhere; the AIDS epidemic has struck; the use of drugs and drink has exploded, for people can no longer live with themselves. Drugs produce suicide. The human wreckage not only leads to tortured lives; it undermines the moral fiber and the economy of nations, especially our own.

Pope Paul VI was mindful of the crisis from the conflict between the moral law forbidding contraception and the need for family planning. He wrote that "it is extremely difficult these days to provide for a large family." And so, he added, "It is extremely desirable that science develop natural family planning" to harmonize true love and responsible parenting.

Pope Paul issued this plea to scientists with trust in God's never-failing providence. His trust was rewarded. The conflict between the good of married love and the responsibility of sexual morality in marriage has been solved. Doctors John and Evelyn Billings and many others have developed a moral method of natural family planning that works. The World Health Organization of the United Nations has confirmed its high reliability and funded the method in a number of countries. Virtually every diocese in this country has a center which teaches natural family planning.

God and creature have provided the solution, but the moral crisis remains. Only a fraction of married people have adopted the method. Why? Have they not heard the good news? Have they not paid attention to it? Have they not believed what they have heard? Or are they not interested in what may well be the greatest gift of divine providence in our time because it is marked as always with the cross of self-control? For the inhuman solution, like all sin, always tempts by promising more than it can deliver, while the way of Christ is always open and honest about the sacrifices and sufferings of the way to true life.

Finally, if we adopt the God-given solutions, and do our best, God will provide. He fed the 5000 who foolishly, as some would think, followed him into the wilderness. His teachings make us understand that we cannot escape sufferings and sorrows; we must choose those from obedience, not those from rebellion. St. Paul says, "Sorrow for God's sake produces a repentance without regrets, leading to salvation, whereas worldly sorrow brings death." The world thrusts inhuman and immoral solutions on us, but we must resist with all our strength. St. John Chrysostom says, "It is possible to love and yet draw back when danger threatens." Will we embrace God's wisdom and providence, or follow the world, which believes only in its own warped wisdom?

There is one problem no atheist will solve, the problem of gaining eternal life. God alone even promises it, and he will give it if we walk with him. Today he will feed us better than he fed the 5000. He will give us the sacrament of his resurrection. In his presence we can find wisdom and the way to life.

''B'' — Eighteenth Sunday of the Year   Ex 16:2-4, 12-15
                                                      Ep 4:17, 20-24
                                                      Jn 6:24-35

CHALLENGING BELIEF IN CHRIST

One day in Jerusalem a man who customarily ate white bread was eating wheat bread. Never had a cat shown interest in his white bread, but now one tried to climb his trouser leg to get a share of the wheat. When given a piece, it chomped on the morsel contentedly. Through the ages, bread has been called the staff of life. It has been the main food of many of the poor through the ages. But like the bread that attracted the cat, it was whole grain bread with the full nutrition the body needs.

Today Jesus calls us to eat the ''whole wheat bread'' of the spiritual life, the true bread of heaven, the staff of life everlasting. Today's Gospel draws us into a dialog that leads us to the Eucharist by enlightening our faith. Let's try to be there with the people questioning Jesus, and enter into the concerns that were theirs, and ought to be ours as well.

The people ask Jesus some crucial questions, questions as crucial for us as for them. And Jesus gave one answer which is a real surprise if you really pay attention to it. When the people asked, ''What must we do to perform the works of God?'' they were really asking, ''What must we do to be saved?'' In answer, Jesus said, ''This is the work of God: have faith in the one he sent.''

Fair enough, so far. Then came the powerhouse question which, boiled down, comes to this: ''Why should we believe in you? What do you do that we should believe you?''

That is a good question. What does Jesus say in answer? The answer is complicated by the remarks about the bread from heaven; but his answer, in the light of subsequent events, comes to this: ''I become the bread of life. I become the Eucharist. I become the Eucharistic sacrifice of Calvary and the Mass.''

Surely, that must make us think. Jesus does not answer by speaking of the healing miracles, or the miraculous feeding with ordinary bread. He refers to the Eucharist as the proof which validates his mission and demands our faith in him.

The word *Eucharist* means thanksgiving. It is a thanksgiving sacrifice to God that takes away the sins of the world. Offering this sacrifice is what Jesus does, and it is why we should believe in him. What better proof can we have of Jesus' identity as the God who is love than his loving sacrifice on the cross? What greater love could he show than to continue to offer this gift for us in the Holy Sacrifice of the Mass, and to feed us with his body and blood in the bread of life?

But what proof do we have that the Eucharist is what Jesus says it is? Jesus answers that question too. He says, ''No one who comes to me shall ever be hungry, no one who believes in me shall thirst again.'' That is Jesus' work and his proof. The Eucharist is its own proof and validation. If we receive the Eucharist worthily, it does for our souls what food does for the body. It gives us pleasure, consolation, strength, spiritual healing, and a sense of life eternal. These things we experience if we bring to the Eucharist a faith that has sculptured our lives into his likeness.

This lived faith is the only acceptable faith. Faith and faithfulness are inseparable. If we have living faith in Christ, we are faithful to his word. To believe in Jesus in any real sense is to live by his word. That is what St. Paul is insisting on in the second reading. Real faith is not empty. It throws out pagan ways and produces a living, breathing image of God. ''Not every man who says Lord, Lord, will enter the kingdom of heaven,'' Jesus once said, ''but he who does the will of my Father in heaven.''

If we live a life worthy of the bread of life, that bread will make us experience its effects. They will be the proof Christ gives us that he is the one sent by the Father, the Incarnate Son of God. If we do not live a faithful life, we may experience nothing. We will lose our appetite for the bread of life. That is an alarming spiritual sign, as it is an alarming sign of poor bodily health to have no desire for food day after day.

The Introductory rites of the Mass and the Liturgy of the Word help us see these truths, and they awaken our hunger for the bread of life. We begin the rites in the name of the Holy Trinity, Father, Son and Holy Spirit. We confess our sinfulness, and ask forgiveness and healing. We sweep into the Gloria, the prayer of praise, as a kind of warm-up for offering the thanksgiving sacrifice. In the Opening Prayer, we ask for what is most appropriate in view of what the Scriptures are about to tell us.

Then we hear the scriptural readings. The Church calls them the other table that nourishes us. Just as, at the Last Supper, Jesus fed his disciples on the revealed word before he fed them with his body and blood, so he does for us.

The Introductory rites, then, are a spiritual ascent by which we enter the Upper Room of the Last Supper. We participate in confessing, repenting, listening, and receiving instruction and inspiration. We move forward in our conversion. We grow in faith, hope and love. We feel awakening in us a longing for the moment we will offer the Father the saving sacrifice and at last come to his divine table and share his divine food.

When Jesus promised the bread of life, so many lost faith and left that he turned to his Apostles and said, ''Do you also want to leave?'' Some Christians do leave, convinced they have valid objections to some teaching of Christ or his Church. Let them instead ask their questions as boldly as the Jews asked theirs of Jesus, and Jesus asked his of the Apostles. The answer may end their problem; or it may point to a problem within themselves, a failure in faithfulness that undermines faith and will be solved only when they walk the way of truth and escape the darkness of sin clouding their minds. We are told of one saint who was challenged on doctrine by a heretical Catholic. The saint told him in answer that what he needed was a good confession. He made it and his problem disappeared.

The Apostles walked the way of truth. That is why Peter could respond to Jesus so touchingly, ''Master, to whom shall we go? You alone have the words of eternal life.'' Would not Jesus be pleased to hear us speak those words as our own when we receive this day the bread he promised that day in Capernaum?

''B'' — Nineteenth Sunday of the Year   1 K 19:4-8
                                                          Ep 4:30-5:2
                                                          Jn 6:41-51

BRINGING JESUS BACK

Jesus promised the bread of life in a synagogue at Capernaum. Near the shoreline there the ruins of a synagogue, and of what is identified as Peter's poor little house, have recently been excavated. So there is evidence a pilgrim can now stand on the very place where Jesus made his promise. At the Last Supper, he fulfilled it and gave a timeless command to repeat it. We are here at Mass to do so.

The Introductory Rites dispose us for the Eucharistic Sacrifice by stirring our faith, longing, and gratitude. In the Eucharistic Prayer our sacrifice will be offered, bringing Jesus to our altar in his real presence. What Jesus promised at Capernaum and gave at the Last Supper he continues to give us.

The Eucharistic Prayer pulses with the words and actions of Jesus. It rings with praise to God for the whole work of redemption; by it our gifts become Christ's body and blood.Let us look at the key parts of the Eucharistic Prayer.

First comes the Preface. It resounds with our thanksgiving. How shall we bring out its significance? There was a woman who used to feed the birds summer and winter, but then she moved away. A month later she returned for a visit. As she left her car, a great outcry descended from the skies, and a large flock of birds, swiftly gathering from nowhere, came sweeping down with excited twirpings and chirpings of alleluia that their benefactress had returned. Shall we show less joy at Christ's return to save us and feed us? The Church hopes not. It expects us all to cry out our praise and joy in the Holy, Holy, Holy. We do it, mindful of the heavenly hosts with whom we sing in unison. The number of Prefaces available have been multiplied by the Church to make us mindful of the many motives we have to be thankful.

After the Preface comes the Epiclesis. It is our earnest appeal to God to stir up his power, consecrate our gifts, and make them the body and blood of Christ, the immaculate Victim of our sacrifice.

The Institution Narrative and Consecration follow: The priest, in the person of Jesus, repeats his Last Supper words and actions, and Jesus accomplishes the very sacrifice he instituted.

Let us pause here over the words of Jesus, "Do this in memory of me." The word *memory* can imply an absence, but as one scholar said pointedly, Jesus is saying just the opposite. The English word *recall* can make the point: It has two almost contrary meanings. The first is *to call to mind;* the second is *to call into one's presence,* as when a soldier is *recalled* to active duty. The meaning of Jesus' words have this second sense: "Do this to call me back."

After the consecration, he *is* back, and the Anamnesis follows. Anamnesis is the word so poorly translated as "memory." Now we make another try. We all cry out the mystery of our faith: Christ has died, Christ is risen, Christ will come again!

You, the people, are meant to understand that the priest is always our voice or Christ's voice. You should attentively identify with him and the words he speaks; but when you are called to raise your own voice, never "muff" it. Express all you have held back during your silent participation.

What the Consecration and Anamnesis have brought about is put into words in the prayer of Oblation or Offering that follows.

The priest, speaking for the whole Church, offers the immaculate Victim to the Father, in the Holy Spirit. The Church urges you to join your hearts to these words and offer yourself with Jesus to the Father.

The Intercessions follow. By these prayers the Church expresses the unity of all her members in heaven and on earth, living and dead. The praise is by all, the sacrifice for all, and the petitions are for all who still need help.

The final element is the Doxology, in which praise of the most holy Trinity rings out once again. You affirm this praise with your resounding *Amen!* This ends the drama of our offering to God. God, in turn, shares the gift with us in the Communion Rite.

We now have four major Eucharistic Prayers, to highlight more brilliantly the riches of our Holy Sacrifice.

The first Eucharistic Prayer is an ancient one. It has the special quality of putting us in contact with our living roots, the saints who are now with God. By their intercession we beg from God a share in their holiness. We turn our hearts to Mary, Joseph, the Twelve Apostles, and many early saints and martyrs. We recall the sacrifices of Abel, Abraham, and Melchizedek, who worshipped our God so long ago. This Eucharistic Prayer helps our faith take strength from the ages.

The brief second Eucharistic Prayer hastens along like us, a people on pilgrimage with Jesus, Son and Servant of the Father. Stripped to essentials, it highlights the sacrifice and Communion of the Last Supper. By reason of its uncomplicated lines, it harmonizes well with the many Eucharistic themes made possible by the rich choice of readings and Prefaces we now enjoy.

The third Eucharistic Prayer features the Holy Spirit and the call to salvation of people everywhere. It recalls that Jesus worked through the Holy Spirit, and asks that he, our Sanctifier, may transform our gifts into the body and blood of Jesus.

The fourth Eucharistic Prayer is the most majestic. Its inseparable Preface begins in the high reaches of the Blessed Trinity, descends into the outpouring of creation, and envisions the angels and the first humans. It ranges through our religious history, from the fall through the ages of sin to the age of the Incarnation and redemption. It beholds always God's radiant and undying love. It looks forward to the age beyond sin, corruption and death, when with the Blessed Mother and all the angels and saints we will raise through Christ-with-us the eternal cry of thanksgiving to God.

May God deepen our faith in and understanding of the Mass, and help us enter more profoundly this day the Sacrifice of Christ, and the mystery of the Bread of Life. Like Elijah in the first reading, at times we feel disheartened by life; but reinvigorated by the Living Bread at Mass, we find strength to continue our pilgrimage to the eternal Mountain of God.

``ABC'' — The Assumption

Rv 11:19; 12:1-6, 10
1 Cor 15:20-26
Lk 1:39-56

THE WOMAN WITH GOD

If you were asked to picture the ideal Christian, would you propose an ascetic who is always fasting and doing penance? Or perhaps someone who spends his whole day doing good works? Or one who goes off to the desert to be alone with God in prayer? Or perhaps a Francis of Assisi, who seemed to love everyone and everything?

Actually, God and his Church have saved us a lot of headwork by identifying the model Christian for us. It's none but Mary. The Church never tires of putting her before our eyes as the perfect disciple of Jesus. Like flowers decking the landscape, the Church has sprinkled her whole year with feasts of Mary.

Let's meditate on Mary along the following lines: Why is Mary the ideal Christian? How are we to model ourselves after her? How can we honor her?

First, then, why does the Church name Mary the ideal Christian? To lay to rest any doubt that the Church does name her that, listen to what it says of Mary: "In her the Church holds up and admires the most excellent fruit of the redemption, and joyfully contemplates, as in a faultless model, that which she herself wholly desires to be."

To begin where we are on this feast of the Assumption, the Church desires what Mary has. She has Jesus, for she is with him in heaven; and she has a full share in his risen life. She has been redeemed, body and soul, for time and for eternity.

But that is only a beginning. Mary was the ideal Christian on earth as well, and in a way, Jesus himself told us why and how. When the unknown woman cried out, "Blest is the womb that bore you and the breasts that nursed you," Jesus replied, "Rather, blest are they who hear the word of God and keep it."

Mary did just that, in an incomparable way. First, she heard the word of God. To hear in this sense means to *hear* and *believe* and *keep* it. Mary's motherhood of God came about through her supreme act of belief. She believed, and then conceived Christ. Elizabeth understood this. In today's Gospel she says to Mary, "Blessed is she who trusted that the Lord's word to her would be fulfilled."

Mary didn't just believe the word of God; she kept it. She lovingly, ardently obeyed it and lived it. She saw the law and the covenant of both Old and New Testament for what it is, a marriage bond between God and his people. God often spoke of it that way, and in Isaiah he says to his people, "As a young man marries a virgin, your Builder shall marry you; and as a bridegroom rejoices in his bride, so shall your God rejoice in you." This promise came about in Mary's body, when God and man became one in Christ. Christ is the Covenant between God and man. Mary is the Ark or container of that covenant which is seen in the vision John records in today's first reading.

Some people look on God's law as a nagging thing; Mary looked on it with sweet joy as the way to please her divine bridegroom. It's no accident that the first time we hear her speaking she concludes, "Be it done to me as you say," and the last time we hear her she gives us her wise counsel, "Do whatever he tells you."

We don't have time to go through all her other admirable qualities: her sublime way of praising God's mercy and might and works and faithfulness; her immaculate conception and lifelong sinlessness; her loving discipleship and her standing faithfully with Jesus crucified till the end; her care for others and concern for the world's salvation; her maternal role in our own rebirth to God. Is it any wonder that the Church sees in her just what it wants to be, and wants each of us to be as far as we can?

But how are we to imitate so sublime a model? Mary is so humble she would be the first one to reassure us we can do it. She might say to us, "I'm only human. What makes you think you can't imitate my faith and faithfulness, my hope and love? I'll always be there to help you. What mother doesn't help her child?"

We can imitate Mary's faith. We believe, as she did, that she conceived the Son of God in her womb. By believing, we conceive him in our hearts, and by serving him we conceive the members of his body. We can imitate her faithfulness. She was conceived sinless, but by our baptism original sin was removed; and even when we sin, we can always start imitating her again. Who can prevent us?

We can hope with her for the resurrection and the eternal life with God which she had to believe in before receiving it. We can believe in God's love for us and providence over us. He does great things for us all. He gives us his Son and his life.

We can certainly do our best to imitate her inspiring example of love. Let's not be so lacking in wisdom as to think we can't imitate our own heavenly mother when Jesus called us to imitate even him and the Father in heaven. We should be humble about it, for we can never be anything like her equal; but humility is the truth, and Truth himself gave her to us as our mother and model, saying "Behold your mother."

Finally, how can we honor Mary? How? Who can count the ways? But I've already described the best way. Aren't we all honored most when someone is so impressed with us that he tries to imitate us? Not only will that well please our Blessed Mother but without doing that we can't please her. Like every good mother, she wants us to be good as she is good, and she wants for us the best of what she has. We gain all that when we imitate her imitating her divine Son.

To please our Mother, we also ask her help. She is the most sublime and powerful of all intercessors with our Lord. Only he is Redeemer, but she more than anyone else was his helper and continues to help him by caring for us. What is more human than to ask our mother to assist us in all our needs? Are we too big for that? In truth, until she gives us full birth into Christ in eternal life, we are still in her spiritual womb. And so we ask her to pray for us sinners "now and at the hour of our death."

Today, we're happy for Mary because she has perfect happiness, and for ourselves because we have such a loving mother and model. We're happy enough to tell the world about her by our songs and our prayers and our words and our way of life. May we have the wisdom and grace to do it forever.

But let's not conclude with forever. Here and now as we offer our Savior in the Holy Sacrifice we can imitate the love with which she offered him on Calvary. And how better receive Holy Communion than by recalling the love with which she took him into her heart? Prepare us, O Mary, for loving communion with Life himself today.

Pr 9:1-6
Ep 5:15-20
Jn 6:51-58

COMMUNION WITH LIFE

Loneliness is an affliction hard to bear, and common as a cold. We can be lonely at home, or in a crowd, because loneliness doesn't so much mean being without a companion as being without a companion who loves, understands, and appreciates us. Jesus must have known loneliness. Who understood him? How many returned the kind of love he gave? And as for appreciation, we know the kind of return he got.

To remedy our loneliness, Jesus gave us the gift of a companionship so loving, so complete, so divine, that none but he could give it. We call this companionship Holy Communion.

It may seem to belittle Holy Communion to call it a mere remedy for loneliness. It is so much more. But realize that loneliness is love calling, and Holy Communion is the beginning of the loving union of God with his people. And this union brings eternity with it, as Jesus makes clear when he says, ''If anyone eats this bread he shall live forever.''

Holy Communion is a paschal or passover meal because it unites us with Christ in his paschal sacrifice. By receiving him, we pass over from sin's slavery to redemptive freedom, from mortality to resurrection life, and from creation to the Creator. The Church urges the faithful to heed the Lord's command to eat his body and blood, providing they have the freedom from grave sin which so holy a Communion requires.

The Communion Rite of the Mass prepares us for a devout reception of the Lord.

The Rite begins when we pray the Our Father together. We ask our heavenly Father for our daily bread, and here we mean to include especially the Bread of Life. We pray earnestly for the grace to be forgiven and to forgive, so we will be fit for the "Holy Things" we are to share.

Then the priest prays an added prayer, the Embolism, pleading for our delivery from all evil and strife, and everyone joins in the concluding acclamation of God's power and glory.

The Rite of Peace follows. We plead for unity in the Church and the whole human family and, at the priest's invitation, express our state of peace with one another by word and gesture.

The Breaking of the Bread is deeply symbolic. With small groups, just one unleavened loaf may be consecrated. It is broken into enough fragments to share with all. This makes it plain that we all partake of the one Bread that is Christ, and in him become one body.

While the priest breaks the bread, all say the Lamb of God, appealing once again for forgiveness and peace. In olden days, the fragment of host that the priest drops into the precious blood was brought to him from the bishop's Mass, as an expression of unity.

The Private Preparation of the priest follows, and all should, like him, turn their hearts to Jesus. Then follows the Invitation to look on the Lamb of God who calls us to share in his saving feast, and we respond with sentiments of lowliness.

We have prepared ourselves, and at last the communicants among us come forward with joy and reverence to receive their Lord and their God.

It only remains for us to ask ourselves what Holy Communion means to us. The saints leave no doubt what it meant to them. St. Augustine marvelled at this gift. He said, "Although God is all-powerful, he is unable to give more; though supremely wise, he knows not how to give more; though vastly rich, he has no more to give."

Once, a Catholic explained to an Arabian prince what we believe about the Eucharist. The Arabian asked how he could possibly believe that God could so lower himself, and added, "We

Moslems have a much higher idea of God.'' The Catholic replied, ''You have only an idea of the greatness of God . . . You do not know his love.''

The saints knew his love, and tried to return it. Once when St. Therese of Lisieux was quite sick, she dragged herself from bed to Mass, and returned exhausted. Another Sister told her she shouldn't exert herself that way, but Therese replied, ''Oh, what are these sufferings to me in comparison with one Holy Communion?''

Padre Pio of Pietrelcina, the stigmatist, said, ''My heart feels as if it were being drawn by a superior force each morning just before uniting with him in the Blessed Sacrament.''

To understand Holy Communion is to know that it is the necessary fulfillment of the Mass. Mass cannot be offered unless at least the priest receives. Communion is also the purpose of the Mass, and the very purpose of Christ's coming into the world. He came to take away sin that separates us from God and one another; he came to unite us to God and one another. He accomplishes it through the Church and her Eucharist. The Eucharist belongs to the Church. It is the Church at its most perfect point of union. As a farmer gathers wheat from the fields into one bread, the Church gathers us from the world into the one Eucharist to be one body with Jesus and one another.

What of those who, for lack of fasting, or any other reason, can't receive? They should make a spiritual communion. Their very presence at Mass is telling the Lord they want him, and he knows it, but they should say so in their hearts. In the days when daily Holy Communion was not allowed, St. Catherine of Siena said, ''When I am not able to receive my Lord, I go into the Church, and there I look at him . . . I look at him again . . . and this satisfies me.'' Be sure that the loving Jesus will supply the needs of those who for any reason are deprived of his Eucharistic body and blood.

It's impossible to love Holy Communion enough. It joins us to

Christ, gives us his love, unites us with one another, implants resurrection life, assures us of eternal life, identifies us with the Son of God, returns us to the Father, gives us strength to overpower sin, and awakens the ardor to serve as Jesus did.

One saint has said that without the Mass, the world would collapse under its load of sins. It seems as likely that without the billion hearts fused by Holy Communion, hatred would tear it to pieces. So for Mass and Holy Communion, thanks be to God!

"B" — Twenty-first Sunday of the Year   Jos 24:1-2, 15-17, 18
                                                                Ep 5:2-32
                                                                Jn 6:60-69

THIS YEAR OF THE LORD

Each time we enter a church we are enveloped by sacred space and time. Sacred space carries us mentally into the presence of God. Sacred time transports us into the days and seasons of the cycle of Christ's mysteries. Vatican II described what this cycle can do for us when it wrote that "the Church opens to the faithful the riches of her Lord's power and merits, so that these are in some way made present at all times, and the faithful are enabled to lay hold of them and become filled with saving grace."

We can better lay hold of these saving graces if we understand the annual cycle of the mysteries of Christ. The cycle is called the Liturgical Year. But where shall we start? Let's start with our Lord's words to the Twelve in today's Gospel: "Do you want to leave me too?" Many had abandoned Jesus because they were scandalized by the mystery of the Eucharist. We have been hearing Jesus speak of that mystery for the last several weeks. By his question, Jesus is informing the Twelve that they must accept the Eucharist or reject him. Peter swiftly accepts, exclaiming, "Lord, to whom shall we go? You have the words of eternal life. We have come to believe . . . .'' And Pope John Paul II has chimed in with the powerful statement, ''Without the Eucharist there is no Church.'' Let us chime in too, saying, ''Lord, we don't want to leave you in any of your mysteries.''

The Mass is the heart of the liturgy. The word means ''the action of the people.'' That was the Chosen People's phrase for worship. Our worship is centered on the Eucharistic sacrifice. The priest stands at the head of the people in the person of Christ, who is present but unseen. The Mass is the building block of the liturgical year.

The primary sacred time is Sunday. It is the original Christian feastday. From the time of the Apostles, it has been called the Lord's Day. Ever since, the faithful have assembled on Sundays to hear the word of God, take part in the Eucharist, and celebrate the paschal mystery of the Lord's passion, resurrection and glorification. Sunday calls us to a day of holy joy and freedom from work. Sunday's sacred time flows from the Mass into our whole day.

The 52 Sundays form the framework of the liturgical year. The year is divided into seasons that unfold for us ''the whole mystery of Christ.''

The sacred year begins with the Advent season, the season of longing for God in Christ, and of preparing for his birth on Christmas. Daily attendance at Mass is the ideal way to participate in the Advent season, and indeed in the whole liturgical year.

At last the Christmas season comes, and we all know how touchingly it re-presents Jesus' birth and childhood mysteries. It is followed by the Season of the Year, which carries us into Jesus' years as a grown man, and into his public life.

Then we are plummeted into the penitential season of Lent. We march with Jesus through the events leading to his passion, we relive the passion with him, and all our burdens become a part of it. We are taught that in baptism we were plunged into Christ's life, and became fellow laborers and sufferers with him.

And then our hearts rise with Jesus on Easter day. Every Sunday celebrates Jesus' resurrection but Easter is the Sunday of Sundays, the "supreme Solemnity" of his conquest of death. Throughout the Sundays of the Easter season we review with the disciples of Jesus his visible manifestations in his risen body. The Easter season closes with Jesus' glorious Ascension. Pentecost Sunday follows, for he did not leave us orphans. He sent the Holy Spirit to guide us and help us discern his presence in his word and sacrament and world.

When the glorious Easter season closes we return to the Season of the Year. We associate with Jesus once again in the events of his public life. Just before the season revolves to a close and opens once again into Advent, Jesus foretells the end of the world and his Second Coming. At his return he will re-channel the cyclic sacred time of earth into the broad and eternal stream of life with God.

In the course of this annual cycle of holy time the Church does not forget her saints. They flash before us one by one to inspire us and pray for us. Having served, suffered, and won the victory, they encourage us by the fact that they were sinners like us, and if they won their way to glory, so can we.

Radiant beyond all the others is Blessed Mary, Mother of God, who is still associated most closely with Jesus and his unfinished task. She is the most perfectly redeemed one, the faultless model after whom the whole Church yearns to pattern itself, and to whom it looks for love, comfort, and intercession.

Let the Mass, the gleaming cornerstone of the liturgical year, be our closing thought. Daily Mass is the blessing the saints have cherished. Are we missing out on this pearl of great price? The sainted Cure of Ars exclaimed, "If we knew the value of the Holy Sacrifice of the Mass, how much greater effort we would put forth to assist at it!" We can respond that we are busy people, but queens are busy too. St. Margaret, Queen of Scotland, and mother of a brood of eight, attended Mass daily with her children.

St. Francis Xavier Bianchi said, "When you hear that I cannot celebrate Mass any more, count me as dead." St. Leonard of Port Maurice, passionately writing about the Mass in his little book *Hidden Treasure,* cried, "O blinded world, when will you open your eyes to understand truths which so much concern you? And you have yet the heart to say, 'A Mass more or less matters little!' O mournful, dreadful blindness!" No, one Mass matters very much. One Mass has the power to redeem the world, but we are its channels into the world.

Each Liturgical Year is the Year of the Lord; each Sunday is the Lord's Day; and every other day is his as well. Whenever we can, let us join Jesus in his Eucharistic action of redeeming the world. After all, while the liturgy is Jesus' sacrifice, it is as well "the people's action," and we are the people of Jesus.

"B" — Twenty-second Sunday of the Year

Dt 4:1-2, 6-8
Jm 1:17-18, 21-22, 27
Mk 7:1-8, 14-15, 21-23

THE HELP EVER AT HAND

A beautiful child was born away from home in a distant country where unrest and riots and terrorist acts never ceased. On his seventh birthday, his father said, "My child, I'm now going to take you to your true homeland, where none of these evils exist. It will be a hard and dangerous journey but if you obey me you will be safe." And so they set out together. At times battles raged around them and the father taught his child how to fall to the ground to escape the flying shells, and how to find shelter when explosives were falling.

They climbed high mountains and crawled along dangerous

passes. If the child picked fruit to eat, his father would tell him when it was poisonous and had to be thrown away. Once, when they lay down to sleep in the noon heat of a desert, the father told the child not to wander. The child woke first, saw water in the distance, and ran toward it. He heard a voice say, "Don't go." He looked, and his father seemed to be sleeping. Struggling with himself, he obeyed the voice and stayed. When the father awoke, he explained that the child had seen a mirage and, had he followed it, would have gotten lost in the desert.

When the father saw the most frightful dangers of all looming ahead, he sang a lullaby. The child would get sleepy and say, "Daddy, carry me for a while," and the father would take the child in his arms, and let him sleep on his heart until the worst was past. They went on, climbing near volcanic mountains spewing fire and smoke. Finally, they topped one mountain, and there below was the most beautiful land anyone had ever seen. The father said, "My child, we have come home." The child exclaimed, "Now all the dangers are over!" The father said, "My child, you were never in danger so long as you obeyed me. For I am stronger than all our enemies."

This story is a parable, the father is God, the child is each one of us, and the dangers are temptations and sins. Like the child in the parable, we were born to God the Father away from home in a troubled land. Born to him by baptism, we were given the beauty of a share in the divine nature. The help of the Father that is ever at hand is called *actual grace*. For, as Psalm 46 says, God is "an ever-present help."

Just as our human nature needs the help of other human beings, our divine nature needs the help of the Divine Being, God the Father. Our human life needs to be provided with food and clothing, light and warmth, knowledge and guidance; our divine life needs spiritual food, needs to be clothed in Christ, needs his light and love, and his teaching and guidance. These supernatural helps are called actual graces because they help us act like children of God. They help us to grow spiritually, and love and serve and make our journey to the Father's house.

By actual grace, God enlightens our minds to see the good, and inspires our wills to do it. Without his grace we are like eyes without light, or bodies without food, or an electric motor without current. That is why Jesus said, "Without me you can do nothing." Not that we couldn't do anything good; rather, we couldn't do anything with faith and charity, and so we couldn't do anything to merit eternal life. That is why St. Augustine said that "man . . . cannot live rightly if he is not assisted by the light of the eternal justice of God."

It is why, in the first reading, Moses makes so much of the law of God, which gives us wisdom and lights our intelligence. It is why St. James says in the second reading that "every worthwhile gift . . . comes from above, descending from the Father." It is why Jesus, in today's Gospel, censures the theologians for replacing God's commandments with their own ideas as if they were divine dogmas. It is why Jesus founded the Church to teach us, and sent the Holy Spirit to be our guide. The Holy Spirit is God himself guiding us by our consciences.

The Australian bishops, writing on abortion in 1988, referred to this inner voice. They said that a woman carrying a child "is assailed by many voices which disapprove of what she is doing. A woman has to be very faithful to her truest intuitions if she is to withstand a persuasive counselor or doctor, and listen instead to the still small voice near her heart."

That still, small voice of God guiding us through life was represented in the parable by the father who was always with his child to guard and guide him, and help him to see things as they really are. The mirage of water symbolized deceitful teaching, which seemed so promising; the poisonous fruit symbolized sin, which looked so good.

As that father was always with his child, God our Father is always with us. Be aware of it, and ask his grace in times of problems, temptations and crises. Open your Bible, pray the psalms, and learn to be forever crying out to God to lend a hand.

Be no more ashamed than a child to keep asking your Father for help, for we are children adrift in a universe beyond our control, and Jesus told us that unless we become like little children, we can never enter the kingdom of God.

We can be actual graces to one another. King St. Louis was an instrument of actual grace when he wrote to his son, "You should permit yourself to be tormented by every kind of martyrdom before you would allow yourself to commit mortal sin."

The child of the parable knew his father was present because he saw him. We know only by faith. In John's Gospel, there is an invaluable help to faith that God is with us. It is Jesus' promise of presence given at the Last Supper. "Whoever loves me," he said, "will keep my word, and the Father will love him, and we will come to him and make our home with him." Say those words over and over daily, and walk with God, our ever-present help.

One more thing about the parable: The father assured his child he would be safe if he obeyed. It didn't sound that way, did it, with shells flying? Yet perhaps that point is the most important in the parable. It symbolizes infinite power against Satan our enemy. If Satan weren't so evil, he would be pathetic. No matter what he attempts he is doomed to defeat, for God is incomprehensibly wise and powerful. God did not prevent the Evil One from engineering Jesus' death, but when Satan thought he had won the victory, he had lost the war. If God, the ever-present help, is for us, who can be against us?

''B'' — Twenty-third Sunday of the Year   Is 35:4-7
Jm 2:1-5
Mk 7:31-37

SICKNESS, SIN,
AND THE HEALING MINISTRY

God sometimes punishes sinners and sometimes heals them. Was the sick man whom Jesus healed in today's Gospel worse than the sinners who brought him? And what of our day? Is the person afflicted with AIDS more sinful than the rest of us? What if that person is a new-born baby? These are the questions that confront us when we deal with sin, suffering, and the healing ministry of the Church.

The questions are given wrong answers even in high places. I will refer only to the best answers from the highest places. Pope John Paul II was asked: Is AIDS a divine punishment? He answered, ''It is difficult to know the intentions of God.''

The Church's 1972 document, *Pastoral Care of the Sick,* states, ''Although closely linked with the human condition, sickness cannot as a general rule be regarded as punishment inflicted on each individual for personal sins.'' To illustrate that, think of the case of the newborn baby. And remember that Christ, who was sinless, suffered for the sins of all; and that we should be prepared to do the same; and that some, though they are not sinless, are innocent enough to be chosen to suffer with Christ for the sins of all. So we are dealing with a complicated issue. We must reflect further.

Certainly, we should be aware there is a connection between sin and suffering, as the Scriptures teach from the fall of Adam and Eve to the last book of the Bible. Science can often trace the connection. It shows how abuse of the body by drunkenness, drugs, and misuse of sex can lead to sickness and death.

It's evident from such studies that God has built into nature a natural corrective punishment for sin. It is meant to help sinners see they are courting sickness and death, both in time and in eternity. Its purpose is not to "get even" with them, but to save them from worse. It is like the correction good parents give their children. God wounds only to heal.

So, we have to distinguish between any direct punishment of a sinner by God, and that punishment which comes through nature itself. Either way, the purpose is always to save from a worse fate.

About AIDS, I would say this: In our country, so far, AIDS has afflicted mostly homosexual persons and drug addicts; but in Africa AIDS spreads like wildfire among heterosexuals who sleep with one person after another.

It is also evident that the innocent often suffer from the sins of the guilty. When a man wounds or murders for money, it is the innocent party who bears the pangs. Suffering is in the world because of sin, but frequently it is not the sinner who suffers. The poor and dispossessed are often the victims of the flourishing. Only at the general judgment will it all be sorted out.

Both mortal and venial sins bring sufferings to ourselves and others. That is very clear, is it not? The venial sins of nastiness, impatience, selfishness, and neglect of our duties bring sufferings to those we love. Yet there is the hidden wound on our own souls every time we sin. And let us remember that mortal sin causes loss of eternal life if one dies in that state. But we should be consoled by the fact that mortal sin is not committed by accident. It consists of doing something grievously wrong with sufficient reflection and full consent of the will.

Now let us turn to healing. Thank God, the Church is not appointed to strike people with punishment, but to work for their healing, and warn of the effects of sin. The Pastoral on the Sick teaches something to which we should listen very carefully: "Part of the plan laid out by God's providence is that we should fight strenuously against all sickness and carefully seek the blessings of good health, so that we may fulfill our role in human society and the Church.'' We are, then, to fight strenuously against all sickness in ourselves and others without pausing to ask whether we are dealing with saints or sinners. We don't raise that issue because, like Jesus, we are appointed to work for the healing and salvation of all.

Today's readings invite us to turn to Christ, the eternal Father's whole ''medicine chest.'' He heals spirit, soul and body. The first reading, from Isaiah, foretells impossible cures. Nothing and no one is hopeless. Christ has begun the curing. It will be completed only in heaven.

But do not think of religious healing simply in terms of the body. The soul is the greater victim of sickness and suffering, and the most often healed by God. Jesus heals hearts by his love and minds by his truth. He frees us from the worst suffering of all, that of enslavement to sin and death.

Much sickness is psychosomatic. A sick heart sickens the body. It leads to loss of energy, heart attack, and even suicide. Suicide is a plague among the young today. One college boy was confused and made cynical by lying values and teachings. He read that all love is mere selfishness, even parental love. Deceived by this nonsense, he lost all hope and all desire for life, and was drawn to suicide. Then, in a flash of religious inspiration, he realized ''Jesus loves me!'' That was a true healing by Jesus, a healing as real as the Gospel healings. It changed the youth's life, and he went on to the priesthood.

In today's Gospel, Jesus is in pagan territory, and the pagans learn to say of him, ''He has done everything well.'' Let us for our part not only offer the same praise, but the greater praise of imitating Jesus, so that those who do not know him may have reason to praise us, and through us be drawn to him.

Now let's prepare to receive the Father's whole ''Medicine Chest,'' the risen body and blood, soul and divinity of Jesus. It is the remedy for both sin and death, and it carries the eternal Father's guarantee.

"B" — Twenty-fourth Sunday of the Year   Is 50:4-9
                                                          Jm 2:14-18
                                                          Mk 8:27-35

THE INNOCENCE-SUFFERING CONNECTION

The "Gospel" means "the Good News." What we hear today doesn't sound too good, at least in part. But the good news of the Gospel must be dug out, like digging gold out of the mud. So let's dig and find the gold.

We have to talk about the cross, but not the cross alone. Let us recall that our Church celebrates the Feast of the Holy Cross as our nation celebrates the Fourth of July. On the Fourth we celebrate our nation's founding and its victories. The flag is still flying. The nation has survived against all its enemies. Similarly, the cross rides high. Christ and we are overcoming the world.

That's what the readings are about. Let's consider them in an orderly fashion. First, the good news is that we have a Savior-Messiah; second, the bad-sounding cross is the noble call to campaign with Christ; and third, the good news is that we can overcome the world.

First, then, the good news is that we have a Savior and Messiah. Through the ages the Jewish people had been awaiting their Messiah. Through many months, Jesus' disciples had followed him but never identified him. Now, Jesus challenges them to say who he is, and Peter at last says it: "You are the Messiah!" We can hardly grasp the electrifying meaning of those words for Peter. The hope of the world had come at last, and he walked with him.

But Peter's joy had just begun to soar when Jesus, knowing that his disciples were now as ready as they were going to be, told them of the cross awaiting him.

What is Peter's reaction? In plain English, I think it could be expressed as follows: "Lord, we've been having a hard time, and you're feeling depressed and threatened. Forget all that and cheer up.'' You heard Jesus' reaction: ''Get out of my sight, you Satan!''

And then Jesus went further. Let me put his message this way: ''All of you — my cross is your cross. Unless you carry it, you can't be my disciple. We're in this together.''

A teenager asked a priest advice about a problem. He described his companions as good kids, but added, ''Once in a while they do things I don't like.'' The teenager admitted going along with them at times, but not without a troubled conscience. So he posed this problem: How can I be my own person without being an outsider? In answer, the priest simply encouraged that teenager ''to be his own person.''

What an opportunity that priest missed to explain to that teenager that he was being called to share Jesus' cross! For that is clearly what he faced. It's not enough to be my own person. A pagan can be that. We are more. We are Christ's, and Christ is God's. Christ is our Master and guide. If we follow the moral whims of our group or gang, we have another master than Christ. To carry the cross means to say *no* to the world which has rejected the way of Christ. Christ carried the same cross. He went the way the Father called him, and accepted the suffering the world inflicts when you reject its false ways. By being faithful to Christ that teenager might well be thrust outside by some of his companions but he would gain the deeper love and respect of friends worth having. Let's look deeper into the mystery of the cross.

The cross is the noble call to campaign with Christ for the redemption of the world. Think of the great leaders in the dark days of human history who battled against the pirates, warlords and other terrorists. Their followers felt privileged to put their lives on the line, to exercise courage and heroism, and labor with those great men for the restoration of civilization and freedom.

The call to the cross, which sounds so much like bad news, is in reality the privileged call of campaigning with Christ for the redemption of the world, and the handing out of the gift of eternal life to all who will heed and respond. What greater privilege could there be? It was the call given to the disciples that day, and it is the call given to us. But we won't accept the call unless we love Christ deeply. We must continue to buttress our lives and our service of Christ day by day.

And if we do that, the Good News is that with Christ we will overcome the world. That is his gift, and it is our joy.

Someone might say to me, "It all sounds good in theory, but where are we going to get the courage and endurance to do it?" The answer is meditation on the passion of Christ. Find there the burning love with which he loved us, and find awakening in you a responding love. A deep prayerful pondering of his love will stir the heart of the hardest among us.

And again, someone might say to me, "All right, I'll do that, but I'm weak. I'll still fail. How can I grow strong?" Do you think Christ didn't foresee such problems? He gives us himself and his strength to carry on.

Last week, in the Gospel, Jesus used his touch and saliva to heal the deaf and dumb man. It was a figure of what he does for us in the seven sacraments. He put himself and his body at our disposal. In baptism, he shares his life with us. In the Eucharist he sends us out with such a flame of love it strengthens us to overcome the temptation of any demon; by the sacrament of matrimony, he heals marriage itself; in confirmation, he breathes into us the might of the Holy Spirit; by the Sacrament of Reconciliation, he takes us back when we allow our weakness to overcome us; through Ordination he makes himself present in the person of his priests. Through the gift of prayer, we can meditate on his ways, and prepare for trial; and by it we can cry out for help in the very midst of our spiritual battles. He has prepared us like soldiers for every battle.

Let us, then, listen to the word of the Lord, and rejoice in the gifts he has given us. Christ has not only come, he has called us to share in the campaign. And be sure he would not call us to carry the cross if he did not know that through his gifts we have the power to do it. In him we can do all things.

''B'' — Twenty-fifth Sunday of the Year

Ws 2:12, 17-20
Jm 3:16-4:3
Mk 9:30-37

DOES PRIESTHOOD OF THE PEOPLE MATTER?

Of the many popes and presidents through the ages, very few have been canonized. A man named Alphonsus, who worked as a doorkeeper most of his life, has been canonized as St. Alphonsus, to be honored by all. Prestige is not the measure of worth in the Church. Holiness is, and to it we are all called.

In keeping with today's readings, our topic will be the royal priesthood of the people. Christians are a priestly people who go out to consecrate the world, to make it all God's temple. That cannot happen without humble service and suffering, as Jesus makes clear.

Jesus comes down from the mount after his transfiguration. To do what? To suffer and die and rise. He goes off on a journey — humble, hidden and unrecognized. Why? Because he is being rejected. He takes along his closest followers, to teach them.

Let us listen, for what he says applies to us. He teaches what it means to be the best, and how we should associate with the least; and finally, his instruction helps us to know the service to which our priesthood calls us.

To rank first, Jesus teaches, we must be last of all and servant of all. The ancient Greeks had a saying, ''Be always the best.'' Jesus tells us how to do that. Wall Street's concept of the best is

wealth, power and prestige. Christ says that to be best is to be the
best servant of all. In that lies the fullest likeness of Jesus, who
said, ''I am in your midst as the one who serves.'' And he did
serve, to the washing of feet, shedding of blood, and giving of his
flesh for food.

One priest was shocked when a successful businessman admitted that he engaged in religious activity because it won him a
prestige he had never had in his business. A pastor who formed a
parish council said the members so wrangled and used strong-
armed tactics that he was better off when he did the work himself.
These disorders are not new. In the second reading, St. James
describes similar problems in the early Church. But new or old,
they ruin work for God.

When we truly serve God, we do it for love, not prestige. St.
Augustine says it is unthinkable to ask any gain for love freely
given except the gain of possessing the loved one. When we serve
Christ, it is Christ we want as reward.

Secondly, pursue friendship with the least, not the greatest.
There is a businessman's calendar organizer with a column en-
titled, Important People, so you don't forget any. Should we have a
Christian calendar with a column, Unimportant People? Or is that
something we'd expect only of Ziggy?

Jesus did not seek out the great. He chose fishermen; and he
holds up a child as symbol of the lowly. At work or play, let us
single out the neglected person, and befriend him.

*Finally and most centrally, understand your royal priesthood
of the people.* First, a negative example. A woman, told by a priest
to hang a crucifix in her home, retorted, ''I can't do that! What
would my bridge partners think when they come?'' She should ask,
''What will Christ think of me when he comes?'' Are Christians so
corrupted by the world's effort to keep God boxed up in the walls of
churches that they no longer believe he belongs even in the Christian home?

Remember that God created the whole world, not to mention

the cosmos. He wants it back! It was robbed from him by sin. He sent Christ and us to get it back.

Remember also that Mass is the Holy Sacrifice by which Christ overcame the world. He overcame it out in the world, on a mount called Calvary. You are here to gain the power to go out in the world and continue his victory. That's what it means to share in the royal priesthood of the people.

The priesthood of the laity is called a "royal priesthood" because it shares in the royalty of Christ the King. Lay people are to exercise Christ's royal power over all creation. By bringing justice, mercy and peace to every phase of human affairs, they offer the whole world to God in marriage, in parenting, in citizenship, in work and play.

By your productive work in the world, you provide the goods and services people need; by your example and the power of your citizenship, you bring moral order into society, and fend for the poor and dispossessed. You call for justice, mercy, charity, and truth in the affairs of the home and the nation.

Authority is a gift of God to help in this service. We elect presidents and hand them authority, not to honor them, but to make them capable of serving us the people. The ancient Greek philosopher, Plato, said that the king is for the people, not vice versa. Isn't that essentially what Christ is saying to all of us? Parents are given authority, not to make their children their servants, but to better serve their children by having the authority to form them into worthy citizens of heaven and earth. All of this should make it evident that if worship at Mass ends at the door of the Church, it is failed worship.

Your royal priesthood of the people has two aspects. The first aspect is the evident one. You are all familiar with the great and necessary role of the laity in offering the Holy Sacrifice with the ordained priest, in teaching Christian doctrine, working in the schools, and carrying on the works of charity. What is less heard of, and in great need of emphasis, is that part of your royal priesthood which is wholly your own as lay people. It is your priestly call to reclaim the world for God through your families, your politics, your every influence.

Does the royal priesthood of the people matter? By the will of God, your priestly role in the world is its hope of redemption. You can understand, then, why one priest said about the laity: ''They're the ones who do the job. A priest is like a coach — we encourage the people to do the work for the Lord.'' The ball is in your court. Are you going to let it gather dust, or run with it at the side of Christ?

''B'' — Twenty-sixth Sunday of the Year   Nb 11:25-29
                                                                      Jm 5:1-6
                                                           Mk 9:38-43, 45, 47-48

THE FIGHT FOR LOVE AND GLORY

Our religion is about love always, even when, as today, it is not immediately evident. For God is love, God created out of love, God calls us to heaven's eternity of love, and God warns us against hell's eternal rejection of love.

We tend to mistake weakness for love, and strength for its lack. A father of three little girls put off taking them to the dentist because they cried at the thought, and so he opened them to worse suffering. A youth who contracted AIDS berated his priest because if the priest had more forcefully given the Church's teaching against homosexuality he might have avoided the conduct that led to the disease.

So, at times one who loves must speak forcefully, as Christ does today. He commands us to adhere to truth and goodness at any cost. He calls us to ecumenism, to innocence, and to faithfulness.

He calls us to ecumenism. God has given his Church the fullness of revelation, but his Holy Spirit works in outsiders as well. In the first reading, Joshua was corrected by Moses because he failed to grasp the way the Holy Spirit worked in the community. In the Gospel, John was corrected by Jesus because he failed to cooperate with a man of good will outside the community.

Experience has helped us develop the following principles of ecumenism. We work with others as far as faith and good conscience allow. We respect goodness everywhere, and respect even an erroneous conscience. But we correct erroneous consciences that cause harm to others. An example is promoters of abortion. For Scripture says, ''You shall not stand by idly when your neighbor's life is at stake.''

Secondly, Christ calls us to innocence. We must avoid sin as worse than disease or death, for it leads to living death and eternal punishment. Jesus spoke in his stark prophetic manner. A poet would put it more attractively. He would say love must remain true in its encounter with vast and craggy obstacles, and its battles with vicious and violent enemies. It must endure and recount many treks, battles and triumphs. How else can it grow and wax strong and amass the evidence by which it believes in itself?

If Our Lord condemns sin so fiercely, why have whole contingents of Christians fallen in with the world in denying so many sins? If they haven't, why is the sacrament of penance in crisis? Pope Pius XII said that ''the sin of the century is the loss of the sense of sin.''

Recall that sin is an offense against God, and God is the one who tells us what offends him. The truth about what offends God is as much a part of revelation as the truth about which acts please him. If we reject the Scripture and the Church's teaching on sin, we endanger our salvation. We are like an alcoholic who denies he has a drinking problem. He cannot be helped. Jesus warned of the ''blasphemy against the Holy Spirit'' which will not be forgiven in this life or the next. Is it not such blasphemy to say that what God has condemned as mortal sin is not sin, and no forgiveness is needed?

We have to live with the fact that the true faith is tampered with even in the Church, and false ways are taught by some on both the left and the right. It has become almost a commonplace to admit there is a crisis in the Church.

In the second reading, St. James cites the sin of businessmen exploiting and cheating their workers. St. James makes their fate frighteningly clear. It is passages such as this which are behind the Church's insistent teaching on social justice.

Innocence requires love of God above all else, so that we will resist sin and its occasions at any cost and use the sacrament of forgiveness when we fail from weakness.

Thirdly, Jesus our Lord calls us to faithfulness against all false teaching. He warns against being led astray, and he particularly warns those who lead astray. That is happening with frequency in the Church today. Dissent against the teaching Church is widespread. How can we hear the Good Shepherd's voice clearly except in the Scriptures and the teaching Church?

The famous theologian, Fr. Karl Rahner, in an address at Georgetown, said that a theologian who is breaking new ground is always in danger of committing heresy, even if unintentionally. Fr. Richard McBrien, a liberal theologian who was corrected by the bishops, cooperated in a praiseworthy fashion. His conduct was in keeping with the following statement in one of his books: ''The impression is sometimes left that theologians are presenting themselves as a co-equal teaching body with the hierarchy . . . This is not being proposed here. The Teaching Church (which is also part of the learning Church) has the responsibility and, therefore, the authority to articulate the faith for the whole Church.'' He concludes that all in the Church are bound to express their faith ''in the light of and in fidelity to the official teaching.'' What Fr. McBrien states is what the Church has taught about itself from the beginning.

In keeping with the work of the Spirit as expressed in the readings today, McBrien stresses in this passage a secondary truth that can be put this way: Before the pope and the bishops present their official teaching, they must listen and learn from everyone in the Church who can shed light on the faith. This is the way it pleases God to bring about development of doctrine, and it is the way the Church functions.

Finally, let us recall that Jesus did more for us than warn against those who would mislead us. He promised the guidance of the Holy Spirit to Peter and his successors. The same Holy Spirit who gave the Ten Commandments and inspired the writing of the Scriptures is guiding the teaching Church. If we listen to the Church, we will hear the voice of the Good Shepherd clearly, easily escape those who lead others astray, go the way of salvation, and be a light for many.

"B" — Twenty-seventh Sunday of the Year

Gn 2:18-24
Heb 2:9-11
Mk 10:2-16

RESCUING SPOUSES
FROM BROKEN MARRIAGES

Police tell us the most wrenching experience in car wrecks is to see lovely little children bleeding and crying piteously, or lying torn and dead. It is similarly wrenching to see marriages, the best hope of society, bleeding and dying, and feel the shaking of the foundations of society. For as Pope John Paul II said, "Mankind's future on earth is bound to the family."

And so Jesus forbade divorce. "Let no man," he said, "separate what God has joined." For as the Book of Esther says, God has "given everything its place in the world, and no one can make it otherwise." And so the Church teaches that no power on earth can licitly approve of Christian divorce and remarriage.

Despite God's law, marriages shatter. And so Catholics ask, "What can I do now that my marriage is unendurable? Are divorced people in sin? Can the divorced and remarried receive Holy Communion? What is an annulment?" I will try to answer.

Let us envision a couple whose marriage is breaking down, and follow the steps the Church counsels. A wife learns that her husband is an adulterer. She wants to do what the Church counsels, so she goes to her pastor. She learns Church Law says that unless her own conduct gave cause for the adultery, she has the right to separate. But she further learns that Christian love and the good of her family urge her to pardon her husband and try to receive counseling with him to save the marriage. If she insists on separation, she applies for Church approval.

Is the separation temporary or permanent? That depends on whether the offending spouse will reform, and the injured spouse will forgive as Christ teaches. One wife was a really bad alcoholic. After years of endurance her husband told her he was separating for the children's sake. The shock brought her to seek the necessary help, and the marriage was saved.

Sometimes there is danger to life and limb of children or spouse. If the danger can't be removed, the Church will grant a permanent separation. When that requires a civil divorce to settle property claims and all legal matters, the Church allows it. Since civil divorce does not dissolve marriage in the eyes of God and the Church, it neither offends God's law nor allows for Catholic remarriage. So a spouse who follows Church practice can be separated and even divorced without sin, and can continue to receive Holy Communion and live a faithful Catholic life.

But sometimes separated and divorced Catholics want to remarry, or do remarry outside the Church. Is there any hope or remedy for them? Pope John Paul II addressed them when he said,

"God does not stop loving those who are separated, not even those who have begun a new, irregular (unlawful) union. He continues to accompany those persons with the unchangeable fidelity of his love, continuously calling attention to the sanctity of the violated rule and, at the same time, inviting them not to lose hope." The Pope goes on to say that the Church imitates God in its care for them, "although preserving the practice, founded on Holy Scripture, of not admitting these persons to Eucharistic Communion." He adds that they should attend Mass, hear God's word, bring their children up in the faith, pray and do works of charity and penance "in order to cultivate God's grace and prepare themselves to receive it." So they are to live the best Catholic life possible until by God's help they find strength to do what is needed to come back fully into his grace and love.

They can do one more very important thing: apply for an annulment, in the hope their present marriage may be consecrated. Please understand: An annulment is not divorce, but a declaration that the first marriage was in fact not a binding marriage.

To understand this, we look at what is required for a valid and indissoluble marriage in the Church. The couple must both be Christians, intend a perpetual sharing of their whole life, be open to having children, and be possessed of the mental balance, emotional maturity, and capacity to make commitments, all of which are necessary for marriage. The marriage ceremony must be in accord with the law of the Church. If they enter into such a sacramental marriage, and consummate it with the marriage act, no power on earth can dissolve that marriage.

If a marriage fails, and the couple apply for annulment, Church officials examine both partners to learn whether any of these essentials to an indissoluble marriage were absent from the beginning. They may learn that one spouse never intended to have children, or lacked a mature capacity to make a perpetual commitment, or even deliberately excluded it. One priest preparing a couple for marriage spoke of the necessary intention of sticking together through everything. The young man said, ''If the marriage goes well, we'll stick it out. If not, what is the sense of it?'' When he wouldn't change his mind, the girl handed him his ring and said, ''I thought you loved me.''

That priest saved her from tragedy. But some marriages proceed with a defective intention of that kind. When an annulment is sought, such defects are often discovered, and the Church can annul the marriage, that is, say that there never was a true marriage in Christ. Be aware that the purpose of the annulment proceeding is not to place blame but to learn whether the Church can declare a marriage faulty and non-binding.

The Church wants kindness and love toward all whose marriage has failed; and it wants earnest efforts to prevent failure by making marriage in Christ excel even that of Adam and Eve who met with all the ardent passion of a sinless love. So just as there is MADD, Mothers Against Drunk Driving, there should be SADD, Society Against Destructive Divorces. There in fact is such a society, and it's the Church, and we should all do our part, especially spouses themselves. And to help, here is *A Baker's Dozen For Spouses*:

1) Be generous to the desires of your partner.
2) Criticize rarely and with love.
3) If you must neglect someone, never let it be him/her.
4) Make your mate shine.
5) Meet like Adam and Eve met the first time — with a sign of affection.
6) A compliment-a-day is more important than a vitamin-a-day.
7) Never both be angry.
8) When wrong, say you're sorry — and settle before sundown.
9) Never, never throw up past mistakes.
10) Pray together and be aware of your oneness in Christ.
11) Never, never ask or give what God forbids.
12) It takes two to quarrel; subtract one.
13) Don't yell unless the house is burning down.

OWN NOTHING, POSSESS EVERYTHING

Some years ago a humorous story was going around about an East German border guard asking his companion, "Comrade, what do you think of this communist system of ours?" The answer came, "Well, I guess I think about the same as you." And the first guard said, "In that case I have the painful duty of arresting you for treason."

Now the question for you is: What do you think of our Lord's call to the wealthy man to give all away and follow him? To answer wisely requires the wisdom found in today's readings. The first says wisdom is worth more than health, wealth and beauty combined. The second tells why: We must live by God's wisdom since we'll be judged by it and eternity hangs in the balance. The Gospel puts before us a special call to live by this wisdom.

The atheist communists Marx and Engels agreed with Jesus at least to the extent of deploring greed. In their *Communist Manifesto* they wrote, "Capitalist employers have stripped of its halo every occupation hitherto honored and looked up to with reverent awe. They have converted the physician, the lawyer, the priest, the poet, and the man of science into paid wage-laborers." Marx seemed to think he could straighten it all out. Did he think that people were going to renounce greed for his sake, when many haven't done it even for God's sake?

Wisdom leads us to ask the key question of life, and the rich man asked it: "What must I do to share in everlasting life?" In answer, Jesus pointed to two ways, the way of keeping the commandments in ordinary life, and the way of the Evangelical Counsels. The man was keeping the commandments, and Jesus loved him for it. Some fail that test. One young man complained to a priest that God commands us like slaves, the way we treat pets.

In answer the priest told this parable: A marine engineer designed and built a splendid yacht. He gave it to his son for his twenty-first birthday and told him how to care for it for his own safety. The son thought, "Dad's too fussy," ignored his instructions, and was killed when his yacht blew up. Most of us are wiser than that. We know that God's commandments are for our own good, and that to ignore them is to destroy ourselves.

The rich man also knew that the wise thing to do was to give up his wealth to follow Jesus the Messiah. That's why he went away sad. He knew it but didn't want to do it.

Jesus continues to call young men and women to the evangelical life of poverty, chastity and obedience in his Church. The world thinks it's tragic. What do you think? Does it test your faith? If so, what do you think of Christ? For as Vatican II said, this way of life "patterns the Christian man after that manner of virginal and humble life which Christ the Lord elected for Himself, and which His Virgin Mother also chose." Can anyone believe in Christ and refuse to believe in his call to chosen men and women to live in his likeness?

Brothers, Sisters and priests who live in the religious state give many special services to the Church. Most basically, as the Council also taught, "the religious state reveals in a unique way that the kingdom of God and its overmastering necessities are superior to all natural considerations." In a way similar to the martyrs they witness that God comes first and his love is powerful enough to make them sacrifice everything.

What the world and the weak of faith find the worst is not the giving up of wealth and power but the sacrifice of marriage. But the more noble we see marriage to be, the higher we see this call must be. The married couple, in their union, are an image of God and they continue his work of creating life by love. But the religious gives up being this image in love to unite directly to God in love. He or she begins here on earth to taste the joys of heaven where none of us will be married except to God in Christ.

Few things in the Church show better than celibacy the New Testament's newness. Christ opened heaven, and this sublime form of life lets its rays shine through dedicated human lives into the world. God is love, and the intensity of celibate love makes even unbelievers wonder, and that is the first dawning of faith.

As Pope Paul VI taught, the Son of God was celibate on earth because it perfectly suited his mission. The married man and woman must by love, duty and obligation give much time and energy to family and its necessities. Christ had to be free to give himself to the whole human family. Priests and religious experience the same calling of love, and therefore feel the need to share Christ's very condition of living. Celibacy is a call to love spiritually and to be fathers and mothers of spiritual life. Religious have worked for the education of tens of millions of children as if they were their own. Priests serve the people of their parish as their family who can call on them day and night.

The total chastity which priests and religious are called to live is an encouragement and support to people in every state of life. If God calls some to perfect chastity, then it is possible by God's grace to live in the other states of life without premarital sex, adultery or other sins against marriage. We all have to live chaste lives; only the manner and degree of sacrifice differ. A single person must be celibate until marriage and a married person must be celibate with all except one.

Christians should learn from this the spiritual element in all love. To a sick or otherwise indisposed spouse, the partner expresses love in more spiritual ways. This helps to teach us that true love is spiritual at root. A married person's love goes out to the partner, but like celibate love it also goes out to God and to all others. St. Jane Frances de Chantal learned this. When her husband was home she turned to him with intense love; when, as often, he was away, she poured out her love to God. After his early death, she became a religious to continue in a fuller way the love of God she had lived in marriage. Her marriage was always in Christ but now it was only with Christ.

Religious work in a thousand ways for the poor, the orphan, the aged, the unborn; they work for social justice and world peace to make our culture a better soil for the Gospel of eternal life to take root and spring up. Christ is called the Father of the world to come, and they deserve to share that title. How can anyone live a richer, wiser life? Pray for vocations, especially in your own family, and if you have the calling, be a vocation.

"B" — Twenty-ninth Sunday of the Year

Is 53:10-11
Heb 4:14-16
Mk 10:35-45

KEEPING THE FAITH BY GIVING IT

A coward has been defined as one who, when he meets danger, lets his legs make the decisions. James and John were no cowards. Jesus had just foretold his passion and they were by no means scared off. They were bold and ambitious. Jesus accepted their boldness but redirected their ambition from bossiness to service.

They wanted to be the generals. In World War One, lieutenants died in droves, but not generals. Generals issued orders; lieutenants executed them. They laid their lives on the line. They were the first out of the trenches into the bullets.

Christ the Son of God was the first out of the spiritual trenches into the battle for salvation. He came on mission from the Father and today's readings highlight his dedication and his call to us to share it. One unmitigated ambition is permitted us: to serve as he did. "The Son of Man," he said, "has not come to be served but to serve — to give his life in ransom for the many."

I'll illustrate the service we owe with a parable. A man with a vegetable garden that grew more than he could eat lived next to a starving family but never invited them to share it. Since there was a saying in the early Church that not to feed the starving is to kill them, what would that make him?

We have a better garden and there is a worse starvation in the world. We have the Garden of the Church which feeds us the food of redemption and the nourishment of eternal life. We must tell the spiritually starving people about it.

Let us look at the people who need salvation, at the way Christ served them, and at our mission to do the same.

Most of the world is in need of salvation. After almost two thousand years, only about one person in five is Christian. Yet Christ is their only Savior, and he commissioned us to the service of revealing him to the world: "Go and teach all nations."

Most of the people we are called to bring to Christ are not atheists. For good reason they already believe in God. According to the word of God, "The fool says in his heart, there is no God." Most people are not fools. The evidence for a Creator registers with them. God can be known with certainty by reasonable people looking at created things.

The Book of Wisdom says that "from the greatness and the beauty of created things their original author, by analogy, is seen." And St. Paul adds that God will punish those who suppress the truth. For "Ever since the creation of the world," he says, "his invisible attributes of eternal power and divinity have been able to be understood and perceived in what he has made."

Modern science adds to the reasons for awareness of God's existence through natural knowledge. The more we learn, the more marvelous and mysterious the cosmos is. One science writer who used to be sure that we'd solve all natural mysteries now doubts that even one atom will ever be fully understood. The cosmos used to look to some as though it always was and always will be. Now we have found that it is a vast system of matter in motion, still going through its birth pangs, and showing signs that one day it will also know its death pangs. By failing to explain itself, and by showing that it too is a creature of time, the cosmos calls thoughtful people to look beyond itself for its Author and Lord.

Besides this proof for God's existence from the world around us, there is a proof from the world within us, wherein God touches the heart. People around the globe and through the ages have shown that they register a law of God written in their hearts. They know good and evil, and sense that God will reward the one and punish the other. But this knowledge of God is weak and incomplete and darkened by sin and mixed with error.

God in his mercy has given us a surer knowledge of his existence than that gained by reason or by the obscure revelation he gives to human hearts. He has given a clear and shining revelation. Through the Chosen People he worked signs and wonders and spoke through the prophets and promised a Redeemer. Then the Son of God came into the world and gave us the new and eternal covenant which reveals God's plan of salvation. And so now we have firm and certain knowledge of God through faith supported by prophecies and miracles and confirmed by the resurrection of our Lord. It is further confirmed by the moral miracle of his Church standing firm for two thousand years in teaching God's truth and resisting errors from without and within.

It is this sure knowledge of faith that we have the mission to spread. St. Paul asked prayers for all people, saying that God our Savior "wills everyone to be saved and to come to knowledge of the truth." To this plea he added his own missionary work, which remains an inspiration and example for us all. Each of us has the obligation to do what we can to spread the Gospel in our own sphere of influence by prayer and service and example.

Christ offered both himself and his service for our salvation, and he calls us in today's Gospel to take him as our norm. Today's first reading is the great Isaian prophecy of how he was to come as the Suffering Servant to give his life as an offering to take away sin. The second reading tells us that like us he knew human weakness and temptation, but never sinned. And in the Gospel Jesus professes himself our servant and our ransom.

Our mission is to imitate him. If called, we should accept a missionary vocation; if not, we owe love, prayers and financial help to those who go. They can't do their work without us.

But there is also the home mission where we live and move and have our being. Read Catholic literature and grow in religious knowledge so you can give reasons for your faith. Talk of what you read and of what you believe. Pray for people without faith or hope. Go to Mass often. Every day offer your day for the intentions in the Redeemer's Sacred Heart. A day not offered is like money not invested. Our Lord said to one mystic, ''An action without an intention would be like a body without a soul.'' Vatican II taught that the laity have a share in the priesthood of Christ, and by their holy actions they consecrate the world to God. Among these holy actions it mentioned expressly their daily work, relaxation, and married life as well as their prayers and apostolic works. For all things become apostolic if we offer them in union with the Heart of Jesus, who was Savior by his carpentry and family life as well as by his Calvary.

We can secure our salvation only by sharing it.

"B" — Thirtieth Sunday of the Year   Jr 31:7-9
                                                      Heb 5:1-6
                                                      Mk 10:46-52

A TREMENDOUS MYSTERY:
CHRIST'S PRIESTS

A priest said to an altar boy, "I can't lose these homily notes. Did you ever lose your class notes and fail a test?" "No," came the answer, but the second altar boy drawled, "He fails his tests without losing his notes." Homily notes don't guarantee a good homily, but here is a sobering note: In a Gallup Poll done some years ago, only about six out of each ten people said that following God's will was "very important."

In those figures a priest sees disaster before his eyes. In today's Opening Prayer we petition that we may do what God asks of us so that we may reach everlasting life. There is no other way to reach it. How do those four out of ten who don't consider keeping God's law very important hope to be saved?

We are Christ's people on the journey to the promised land of eternal life described in parable form in the first reading. It is Christ the Good Shepherd whom we follow there. Though he was blind, Bartimaeus sensed this when he heard that Jesus was passing. That's why he wouldn't shut up. He asked for sight to see Jesus, he saw him, and he followed him to find everlasting life. Together with sight for his eyes he got faith, the eyes of the spirit, and that was the greater gift.

Bartimaeus made a great act of faith, but in one sense he had it easier than we do. Christ has ascended to heaven and has given us the pope, bishops and priests to stand in his place to carry on his work of prophet, priest and king.

The second reading tells us that a priest is called and chosen by God. Pope John Paul II called the Catholic priesthood "a fascinating mystery and a tremendous mystery.'' The Pope said that as Pope he is vicar of Christ, but as priest he and every priest acts ''in the person of Christ.'' That is to say that the Pope is vicar because Christ is as if absent, and he the Pope acts *on behalf* of Christ; but the priest is priest only because in him Christ is *present and acting*.

Ponder the following as a possible miracle: A priest begins Mass. His appearance changes. Christ stands before the people. A great miracle? Yes, but in a way it does not equal the unseen wonder in every priest at every Mass. The priest acts in the person of Christ. How else could he say, ''This is my body,'' and bring about the offering of the Holy Sacrifice?

I invite you to follow me through the ordination of a priest to get inside this mystery. When a man feels called by God to the priesthood, he may struggle for or against the call, because he doesn't want to give what it costs, or because he feels so unworthy of such a call. For as the second reading says, he is beset with his own weaknesses and his own sins.

If the call wins out, he talks to a priest who sets things in motion. If he is accepted into the seminary, the Church begins a long study of his gifts of holiness and all other qualities. This study will go through the years of preparation, right on into the ordination ceremony itself, to test his worthiness.

The years of study go on. As he approaches ordination to the diaconate, he is called to make a public commitment to holy celibacy. His whole life is about to be consecrated to the Lord and the Church. After he is ordained a deacon, he begins to pray the Liturgy of the Hours daily, and to perform the other works now expected of him.

Finally the day of ordination to the priesthood arrives. With his fellow deacons he presents himself to the bishop in the church of ordination. There before all the faithful the bishop asks the priest who presents them, ''Do you judge them worthy?'' The priest responds, ''After inquiry among the people of Christ and upon the recommendations of those concerned with their training, I testify that they have been found worthy." The bishop then invites the people present to confirm this judgment by a word of their own.

In the homily that follows the bishop addresses the relatives and friends of the candidates. He says that while God has made his entire people "a royal priesthood in Christ," he also chose certain followers to carry out a public priestly ministry in the Church in his name for all mankind. They continued his work as Teacher, Priest and Shepherd. The bishops of today are their successors, and the priests share in their priestly office to assist them. "By consecration," the bishop says, "they will be made true priests of the New Testament, to preach the Gospel, sustain God's people, and celebrate the liturgy, above all, the Lord's sacrifice." Then he instructs the candidates in the priestly duties of sanctifying, consoling and uniting the people of God.

Here the bishop asks the candidates once again to freely state their willingness to be ordained and to serve, and to obey their bishop, and he listens to their answers.

At last the solemn moment of ordination arrives. On each in turn the bishop lays his hands in silence. All the priests present do the same. And in the prayers of consecration that follow, the bishop petitions God to accept them. He sums up the prayers at one point when he says, "Almighty Father, grant to these servants of yours the dignity of the priesthood." And now the Church is blessed with newly ordained priests who concelebrate with their bishop the Mass that follows.

The priestly ministry is sacred, solemn, mysterious and demanding. It takes courage to preach the Gospel of faith in an age when people prefer their own opinions, and bravery to preach the moral teachings of Christ when many prefer to have themselves for a guide. It takes much prayer and sacrifice to walk the holy path, and endless self-denial to serve in the likeness of Christ. But a man who is not willing to do all this should never be a priest. It is part of the call Christ gives.

There is a serious shortage of priests. It will end when priests show forth the selfless, loving, fearless image of Christ in them. And when parents make their homes the ''little churches'' that popes have called them. You parents share in your own way in the priesthood of Christ. You instruct your children in prayer by praying together, and in the faith by teaching it and by living it out before their eyes. If we all live more priestly lives, and pray more for vocations to the Sisterhood, Brotherhood and priesthood, we will soon have the vocations we need.

''B'' — Thirty-first Sunday of the Year   Dt 6:2-6
                                                           Heb 7:23-28
                                                           Mk 12:28-34

THE PEOPLE DEVOTED TO LOVE

A woman learned from her brother that a friend of theirs was dating a girl regularly. ''How often does he see her?'' she asked. ''About twice a week,'' he replied. ''He's not serious!'' she concluded. Then there was the boy who knew his sister was engaged and asked, ''When are you thinking of getting married?'' The answer came in one word: ''Constantly.''

Does the nature of love between a man and a woman apply to our relationship to God? How does Christianity help us live a life of love? Are there any special helps to keep us focused on love as the norm of our religion? Since today's Gospel is about love, I invite you to reflect on these questions with me.

First, does the nature of love between a man and a woman apply to our relationship to God? It certainly does. God taught the Jews to see Israel as the bride of God. The first reading, which is from the Old Testament, quotes the command to love God with all one's heart and soul and strength. To this day a devout Jew is bound to repeat these words every morning and evening. How many times he does so in between is left to his devotion.

Jesus named this commandment to love God the central one of all. Let's examine it. "Love the Lord your God with all your heart." If our heart is attached to God, it seeks him constantly. "Love God with your whole soul." The soul is where our depth of commitment lies. If our soul loves God, it commits all it has to him. "Love God with your whole strength." Our strength is the power of action. We commit it all to God. Jesus went further by adding another word: "Love God with all your mind." The mind is the power to know God and his creation. We give God our mind by praying always as Jesus taught us.

This is the love that we Christians are called to offer the Holy Trinity, through Christ the bridegroom of the Church and of every Christian soul. Whether workers or presidents, we're not too busy to do it. The favorite hymn of President John F. Kennedy was the one that begins, "O God of loveliness, O Lord of heaven above, How worthy to possess my heart's devoted love." To answer our question, then, the love between a man and a woman is a school of love that is surpassed in our love of God.

When the theologian asked which commandment was first, it wasn't an empty question because the Jews had 613 commandments, laws, statutes, ordinances and observances. But take note that Jesus went on to answer an unasked question: "This is the second, 'You shall love your neighbor as yourself.' " This command was in the Scriptures, but it was a burst of revelation to raise it above 611 other obligations and put it next to the love of God.

Jesus later made this second commandment far more powerful. "Love one another," he said, "as I have loved you." That staggers us. How can we do it? Somehow we can do it with the help of his Holy Spirit. Jesus went still further when he said, "What you did for one of these least ones you did for me." He so linked and fused love of neighbor with love of him we can't separate them.

Let's look into this deep mystery. What we do for others we

do for Jesus because he shared our human nature; but also because he lives in his members. But what of non-members? If we show love for them, they may become his members, and then we've done even more for Jesus. What a mystery! But there's encouragement here: As long as we're loving others rightly we're loving God.

Second, how does Christianity help us to live this life of love? We know of many helps, but today I want to stress that the commandments and the other laws help us to live a life of love. This comes as a surprise to those who dislike laws, so let's take a clear example. Jesus gave us his body and blood as the sacrament of love and resurrection. He said, "Whoever eats my flesh and drinks my blood has eternal life, and I will raise him on the last day." This gift is so great and so necessary you'd think no more need be said. That's true of some. You find devout Catholics at daily Mass. Yet the Church has found that many still sinfully neglect the love they owe the Eucharistic Lord. So the Church has given the precept that we must confess if necessary and receive Holy Communion at least once a year, and that during the Easter season if possible. What the Church is surely doing is saying that to do less is to grievously sin against the love of God the Son and the salvation he gives us in Holy Communion.

The Ten Commandments too are helps to love. They command us to love God at least enough not to put anyone before him, and to love every neighbor at least enough not to lie to him or rob him or ruin his marriage or murder him.

Some folks dislike any commandments and orders. They only want to love spontaneously. That's unreal. Ask a mother how her infant would fare if she only loved and served him when she felt like it. Who feels like getting up at two in the morning to quiet or nurse a child? All love is like that. Love calls for the works of love even when we don't feel like doing them. We do them because our love is greater than our feelings. Spontaneity and impulsiveness belong in love, but people who want to do everything that way haven't grown up. One psychiatrist who has studied neurotics says that "In many respects, the psychopath is the very model of the impulsive style." Faithfulness to love requires that we moderate our spontaneity; successful living requires that we blend it with self control. God's law wisely guides both mind and will to do the blending.

Finally, are there any special helps to keep love the norm of our religion? The answer is: Make Jesus the norm of every law and every decision. When we have a conflict of duties or any hard decision to make we ask ourselves, "If Jesus were in my shoes, what would he do?" When we ask that, we may get clearer answers than we like, because confusion sometimes comes from our reluctance to accept weighty tasks.

We can rid ourselves of that reluctance by cultivating devotion to our Redeemer's Heart. Union with his Heart makes our hearts stretch more and more to the breadth and depth of his loves and concerns. And if we keep at it, we will come to the day when we really are in every way the people devoted to love. We'll know when we get there, because then we won't need the commandments any longer, just as people who lovingly go to Mass daily don't need to be commanded to go to Mass on Sunday.

"B" — Thirty-second Sunday of the Year   1 K 17:10-16
                                                          Heb 9:24-28
                                                          Mk 12:38-44

HOW TO LIVE THE MASS

A doctor who had seen much of life and death belatedly became a priest. One day at Mass he told his congregation that no one there present would ever cease to exist. Life would be changed but not taken away. Therefore, he said, they had better think seriously about the importance of their religion. Yet in one poll, more than seven in ten Catholics said that their religion was "not so important."

How could they possibly say that? What do you say? Is religion not so important, or the most important of all? Only if we say "most important of all" are we thinking as Catholics, thinking as Jesus Christ taught. When we stand at the judgment seat of God will anyone think in any other way?

Let's make a comparison. Surely, none of us would deny marriage is very important. Marriage is the union of love with your spouse for life, and you give life. Religion is our marriage with God. We are joined to him in love, and he gives *us* life. And if we are faithful he will give it forever.

Jesus taught us religion is important enough to die for, and there is nothing more important than that. And die for it he did.

I give this introduction because the readings today are about sacrifice. Two widows sacrificed their livelihood; Christ sacrificed his life. Now it is our turn to sacrifice, but unless we think with Christ and his Church we'll fail to give what's asked of us, and that will put our eternal salvation in danger.

So I will answer three questions: What is sacrifice? What is the Sacrifice of the Mass? How do we live it out in our lives?

First, what is sacrifice? Sacrifice is giving to the Lord. To make a sacrifice is to make a thing holy by offering it to God. A chalice is holy not because of its precious metal or fine art work, but because we consecrate it and set it aside for God.

The three readings describe three sacrifices. The widow of Zarephath made a sacrifice of the food she had to live on to feed the man of God. The widow in the Temple sacrificed the coins she had to live on to support the worship of God. Christ sacrificed his life to win all people to salvation in God.

Secondly, what is the Sacrifice of the Mass? It is the sacrifice in which Jesus continues to offer himself to the Father as he did in his sacrificial death on Calvary. It is the same priest, Christ himself, and the same victim, his body and blood under the appearances of bread and wine. It is therefore the same offering, but now in an unbloody manner. Christ died once, but every time we offer the Mass he is offering to God the Father himself and his history of sacrifice on Calvary. We the Church join in. We obediently accept with Jesus all that the Father asked of him for our salvation, and we receive it for our redemption.

As Priest, Jesus intercedes for us still; as Victim, he continues to offer his body as it was on Calvary, and as it is now in the Eucharist, risen and glorious, but forever marked with the five wounds of his sacrifice. He prays for us and nourishes us with his body that we may have "the freedom of spirit and the health of mind and body to do the Father's work on earth."

We might compare Calvary to the Wedding Day, on which a bridegroom gives himself to his bride in the wedding rite, and Mass to the days that follow when he continues to give himself to his wife. The gift is the same, but the manner of giving is different. Christ, and we his Church, continue to offer him to the Father for our salvation, and that is sacrifice; but no longer is there any shedding of blood, for the manner differs. Jesus is now in heaven, the sanctuary of eternal life, continually offering himself to God on our behalf. The distance between heaven and earth closes in the mystery of the Mass. At the consecration Jesus is present with us, and present in heaven, and we are with Jesus co-offering him to the Father, offering everything he is, and everything he was and did on earth, especially his Calvary.

Thirdly, how do we live out the Holy Sacrifice in our lives? Recall that his Sacrifice was offered not in a church, but out in the world. That is where we too do the will of God, and live out our self-offering with him. We receive him in the Eucharist and carry his life back out into the world to love, serve and consecrate the world to God as he did on Calvary.

When the two widows gave their livelihood, they were really

giving themselves as Christ gave himself. That is the meaning of gift-giving. We continue his sacrifice wherever we live in fellowship and love, for without sacrifice there is no love. Even in baseball there is sacrifice. When a player bunts to give another player time to gain a base it's called a sacrifice, because the bunter usually can't make it to first base.

To understand what our sacrifice should be, recall that when Jesus came into the world he said, "As is written of me in the scroll, I have come to do your will, O God." This is what Jesus' real sacrifice was, to do the Father's will. Jesus did not make a cross for himself and hang himself on it. Rather, he did the will of the Father, preaching and teaching the truth, calling people to love and obedience and repentance. And he accepted the consequences, he endured what men did to him for doing the Father's will. This is what the Father wanted of him.

It is what the Father wants of us. Our sacrifice is to consecrate our lives to God by living the teaching of his Son and his Church, and accepting the costs and the consequences. It is to show faithful love to God and one another, husbands and wives, parents and children, friends and co-workers and fellow citizens. In these ways we carry out the works of love and obedience. That is the living sacrifice God calls us to. The animal sacrifices of the Old Testament were symbols of Christ on Calvary and of our own sacrifices. Animal sacrifices have gone the way of history, but we still have to walk through history offering our own Mass.

Everything that suffers and dies in us as we move through life we unite with the blood of Christ. Every way we struggle to grow and everyone we help to grow we join to Jesus' resurrection. In the Mass Christ transports the Last Supper and Calvary and Easter into our midst so that we may share his love, life and victory. Union with him in his Real Presence in Holy Communion fortifies us for the task. Let us pray to be faithful in making our lifelong priestly offering in and with Jesus.

"B" — Thirty-third Sunday of the Year   Dn 12:1-3
                                                                    Heb 10:11-14, 18
                                                                       Mk 13:24-32

DEATH, JUDGMENT, HEAVEN AND HELL

They tell the story of an atheist travelling in Ireland who fell into conversation with a young girl. "I suppose you believe the whale swallowed Jonah," he mocked. "I do," she said. "How'll you ever know for sure?" he pressed. "I'll ask him in heaven," she replied. "And what if he's not there?" "Then you ask him."

This is the season of endings and approaching endings, the end of the warm season, the end of the year, the end of the liturgical year. In the realm of faith, the readings turn us to the last things, to history flowing out of itself into eternity, to resurrection and judgment, heaven or hell. These are the inescapable finale for all the children of Adam. They will happen to those who believe and to those who don't believe. Those who did not believe in God will stand before God and be judged. Those who did not believe in hell will learn how wrong they were.

Resurrection and judgment, heaven and hell are among the foundations of biblical and Catholic faith. They are taught throughout the New Testament. In this life people escape into drugs, drink and dreamed-up ideas of reality, but in the end reality itself will be inescapable.

Our Lord said clearly that after the last judgment, the evildoers "will go off to eternal punishment, but the just to eternal life." St. Augustine said that some grieve over the idea of eternal punishment and say it won't be so. But he points out that Christ used the same word for the duration of hell as of heaven, and so it is a fond fancy to imagine that punishment is only for a time but heaven is forever. However, he adds, if it helps you, you may suppose that God's pity reaches down to give some alleviation and periods of respite even in hell.

It is a dogma of the faith that those who die in mortal sin enter an eternal hell. At the Second Vatican Council in 1964 the bishops of the Church said, ''Since we know neither the day nor the hour, we should follow the advice of the Lord and watch constantly so that, when the single course of our earthly life is completed, we may merit to enter with him into the marriage feast and be numbered among the blessed, and not, like the wicked and slothful servants, be ordered to depart into the eternal fire.''

If we need an escape clause, recall that we hope and pray all will be saved. The Church has never defined that anyone, even Judas, is in hell. But since various mystics have had visions of many falling into hell, we ought not to take unwise positions.

Karl Rahner and Herbert Vorgrimler explain the issue clearly in their *Theological Dictionary*. They assert that ''the dogma of hell means that human life is threatened by the real possibility of eternal shipwreck, because man freely disposes of himself and can therefore freely refuse himself to God.''

The point is that God has given us such dignity that he won't force our wills. He leaves us free to reject even him and his eternal home. Our freedom, discernment, choices and actions have eternal consequences, and we are told this beforehand.

Fr. John McKenzie says in his *Dictionary of the Bible* that ''The great truths of judgment and punishment are firmly retained throughout the New Testament and no theological hypothesis can be biblical which reduces the ultimate destiny of righteousness and wickedness to the same thing; the details of the afterlife, however, are not disclosed except in imagery.''

One of the images of hell is that of fire, but its real nature may be the fire of spiritual bitterness and remorse at one's own folly. By nature, our wills long for God; by mortal sin rebels reject him, and so there is this torture of being pulled in two directions. Theologians say that hell involves this pain of loss of God, which is the worst part of it, plus a pain of sense. What is this pain of sense? We do not know. It may be similar to the pain of sense we experience whenever we misuse creatures in any sinful way. Those in hell will never cease to misuse creatures, just as they will never cease to reject God. If this explanation is correct, hell is completely a product of creatures, and not of the Creator. They are there because they hate and reject God. In a sense, they are there because they want to be. We see similar forms of alienation between persons here on earth. God made neither angel nor human being for hell. Hell is the refusal to come home to the Father.

If we are faithful, this reflection on the last things is one of sober hope and consolation. Jesus is telling us that present trials will continue only until he returns. Or, we might add, until we return to him by death. For we should be perfectly aware that the end time has come for many before Christ's return, and may for us. By the time of this Sunday next year, one or many of us may have met the end time. The simple fact without exaggeration is that we don't know the day or the hour. The only way to be prepared is to live today as the last. During the Cuban missile crisis many people rushed to confession. We shouldn't need such a crisis to prepare ourselves. "Today is the day of salvation." We're not assured of another even without a crisis.

A person once asked St. Thomas Aquinas how she could be saved. He said, "By willing it." That's all we have to do. By one offering Christ has given all we need to be sanctified if we cooperate.

The end of the Liturgical Year is inventory time. The *Wall Street Journal* reported that more businesses fail because of poor record keeping than for any other reason. They fantasize that they're doing well because they haven't been taking stock, and crash! they're bankrupt. Our Lord is calling us to take stock. Do a practice run of your final judgment. If you prove to be bankrupt, there is still time to earn new spiritual dividends by penance, repentance, confession, Holy Communion and good works.

But make it a reliable practice run or it will only be a further delusion. Compare your beliefs and practices with what the Scriptures and the Church teach, and amend what needs amending.

Actually, we should each do a practice run of our final judgment every evening. We call it an examination of conscience. Don't go to bed without one. Don't fail to conclude with an act of contrition. With a good life and a good conscience we will look to the last things with some of the joy that Mary had when she thought of going home to her Son and the Father and the Holy Spirit forever.

"B" — Thirty-fourth Sunday of the Year   Dn 7:13-14
The Feast of Christ the King   Rv 1:5-8
                                                                              Jn 18:33-37

THIS PUZZLING KINGSHIP OF CHRIST

Today we honor Christ our King, but his is a puzzling kingship. Do you understand it to your satisfaction? Is he king of this material world or only of its spiritual aspects? What is the nature of his reign? What is the shape our loyalty should take, and what are the duties we owe him? If he is an all-powerful king, why is the world in such a mess?

The place to look for answers is in the word of God. What does it tell us? The Gospel reveals that Jesus is the eternal Son of God who became man of the Virgin Mary. As man he became not a king but a carpenter, prophet and victim for sin.

St. Paul puts this in cosmic language in which he tells us that though Christ was "in the form of God . . . he emptied himself, taking the form of a slave, coming in human likeness." And as a man, "he humbled himself, becoming obedient unto death, even death on a cross.'' That is a summary of Christ's mortal life, but then, Paul adds, God exalted him to such heights that every knee should bend to him and every tongue confess him Lord.

Paul here makes an illuminating contrast between the possession of power and the use of power. Christ possesses the power of God, but as man he shunned the use of that power. He had come to serve. He lived on this earth like a king in the guise of an ordinary citizen, refraining from exercising his right to command. But after his resurrection his glory and power became evident, and to it all owe submission.

Christ himself explained his lowly manner of acting. At the Last Supper, after washing his disciples' feet, he said, ''You call me 'teacher' and 'master,' and rightly so, for indeed I am.'' But he added, ''I have given you a model to follow, so that as I have done for you, you should also do.'' Even more plainly, as he says in Luke, ''I am among you as the one who serves.''

Now when a king takes to serving his servants, things get complicated if not confusing. To prevent our confusion from going too far, Jesus foretold his betrayal and added, ''From now on I am telling you before it happens, so that when it happens you may believe that I AM.'' Don't miss those two words, ''I AM.'' Let's take a deep breath and let them register. When God sent Moses to Pharaoh, Moses asked who he should say sent him. God replied that he should say, ''I AM sent me to you.'' Here, just after he had washed his disciples' feet, Jesus is clearly identifying himself as God, as King of kings and Lord of lords.

To the question, is Christ King of this world, or only of its spiritual aspects, the answer is clear: He is in every way King of this world and of all worlds. He asserted it himself, after his resurrection. ''All power in heaven and on earth,'' he said, ''has been given to me.''

What, then, is the nature of his reign, the manner in which he has chosen to use his power or refrain from using it? Jesus gave the answer in his exchange with Pilate: ''My kingdom does not belong to this world. If my kingdom were of this world, my subjects would be fighting to save me." He is telling Pilate he will not use force and armies in the way of this world's kings. Earlier, when Peter raised a sword to prevent Jesus' arrest in the garden, Jesus said to Peter, "Do you think I cannot appeal to my Father, and he will at once send me more than twelve legions of angels?"

Normally, kings are raised on a throne, and from there they rule. Jesus described the kind of throne he would use, and the power he would use from it by these words: "When I am lifted up from the earth I will draw everyone to myself." His throne would be his cross, and the power he chose to use was the power of his love manifested in his pierced Heart. He is the King of Love, and this most tender and mighty of all powers is the one by which he chose to govern and redeem us all. He evokes from us the freely chosen response of loving and serving him in return. That his power of love will not fail in its effect he assured us at the Last Supper when he said, "In the world you will have trouble, but take courage, I have conquered the world."

What, then, is the shape our loyalty should take, and what are the duties we owe? Jesus answered that question in many ways. I select two. He taught that the greatest of his kingly commandments is to love God with utmost passion; the next greatest is to love one another as he has loved us. We owe him and his the loyalty of love beyond measure.

What are the duties to which love calls? In answer, he told us that on returning as King to collect his faithful sheep, he will find our fidelity etched in a whole stream of works of love: "I was hungry and you gave me food, I was thirsty and you gave me drink, a stranger and you welcomed me, ill and you cared for me, in prison and you visited me." Here we see him fusing the two commands of love into one. What we do to others we do to him.

It's instructive to recall here what a king of this world said about the fidelity owed to our King of kings. King St. Louis of France wrote these words to his son: "Keep yourself, my son, from everything you know displeases God, that is to say, from every mortal sin. You should permit yourself to be tortured by every kind of martyrdom before you would allow yourself to commit a mortal sin.''

Why is the world in such a mess? Not because Christ is not exercising his power of love, but because many of his subjects are not exercising theirs. ''Love is patient.'' He is patiently awaiting their change of heart. In the meantime, ''the world as we see it, disfigured by sin, is passing away.'' Only at the end time, after he has destroyed all his enemies, including death, will he separate the wheat from the weeds, and the sheep from the goats, and gather them to himself. Then his work as Son of Man will be done, and he will eagerly hand over the kingdom to God his Father, and God will be all in all.

Today is the day to renew our allegiance to our King of kings, and to faithful service in his kingdom: O Jesus, through the Immaculate Heart of Mary, we offer you our prayers, works, joys and sufferings of this day and every day in union with the Holy Sacrifice of the Mass throughout the world for all the intentions of your Sacred Heart.

I will repeat those words of dedication, and invite you to pledge them with me now . . .